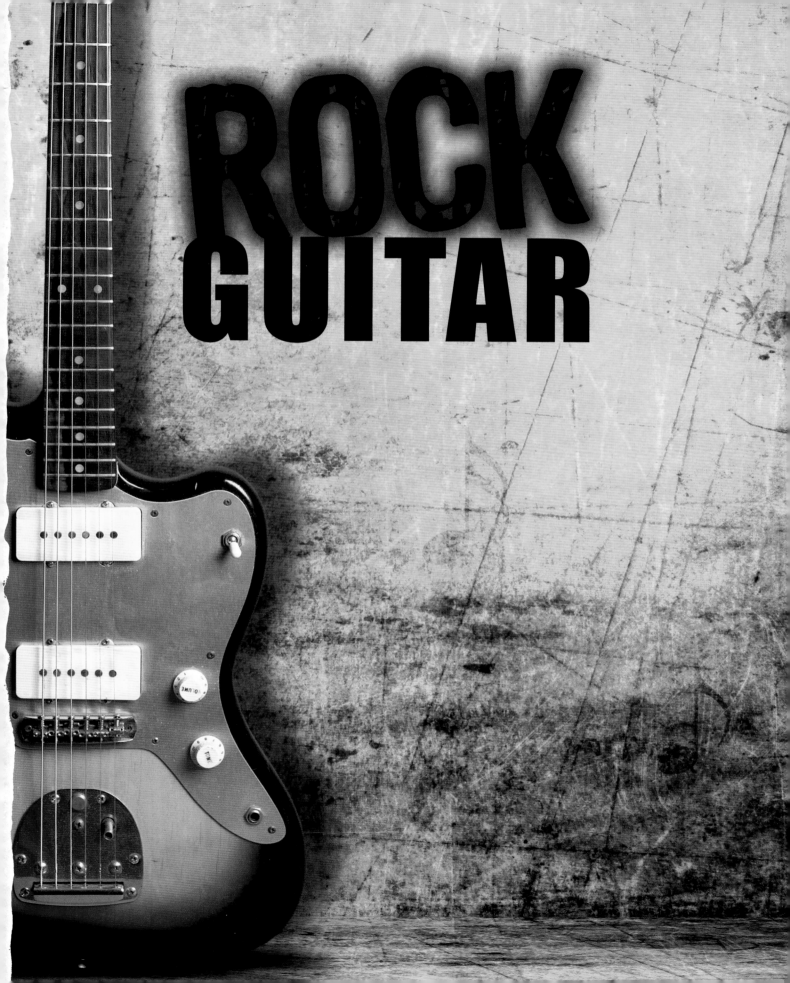

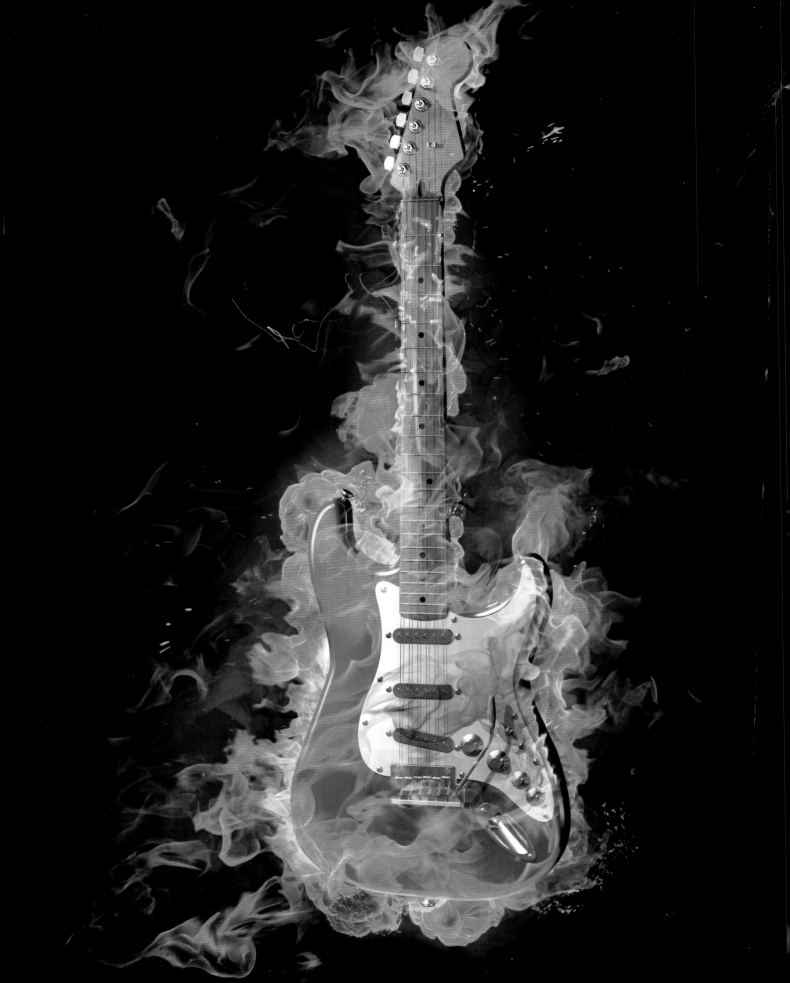

ROCK GUITAR

Learn to play like the rock legends!

Bath · New York · Singapore · Hong Kong · Cologne · Delhi
Melbourne · Amsterdam · Johannesburg · Auckland · Shenzhen

First published by Parragon in 2011

Parragon
Queen Street House
4 Queen Street
Bath BA1 1HE, U.K.

www.parragon.com

Copyright © Parragon Books Ltd 2011

Designed, produced, and packaged by
Stonecastle Graphics Limited

Designed by Paul Turner and Sue Pressley
Text by Jacob "Quist" Quistgaard and Nick Freeth
Original music notation by Quist
Edited by Philip de Ste. Croix

ISBN 978-1-4454-3818-4

Printed in China

Photographic credits:

© **Shutterstock.com:** Mohammad Fariz Abdullah 36 (left); alias (graphic panel) 20, 24, 32, 37, 40, 52, 61, 69, 77, 81, 85; Silvia Antunes 13 (left); Ryan Rodrick Beiler 15 (right); chris87 19 (right); Daniel DeSlover 96 (right); gcluskey 39; Andreas Gradin 95 (left); haak78 7 (above), 12 (below left), 27; INGAJA 1; javaman (background) 4–5, 26–27, 38–39, 42–43, 46–47, 50–51, 58–59, 62–63, 74–75, 90–91; jcjgphotography 9 (below); jiggo 12 (above left); Kayros Studio "Be Happy!" (guitar) 4–5, 8–9, 14; Lia Koltyrina 87 (left), 94; Aija Lehtonen 23 (right); Sean MacD 13 (above right); Mark III Photonics 7 (below right), 15 (left), 83 (below); Girish Menon 44; Mikhail 2; Randy Miramontez 77; Dana Nalbandian 81; Narcis Parfenti 10 (above); pashabo (background) 21, 25, 29, 33, 41, 53; Photonly 12 (right); Ra Studio 93; Semisatch 45 (inset); Ferenc Szelepcsenyi 20, 21, 73; Ana-Maria Tanasescu 44, 79; TDC Photography 51 (right); VolkOFF-ZS-BP 10 (below); YellowPixel 71 (left); Faiz Zaki 7 (below left), 49.

© **Getty Images:** Stephen J. Cohen 59 (left); FilmMagic, Inc/Jeff Kravitz 25 (right); Juan Naharro Gimenez 45; Walter Iooss Jr 28 (right), 41 (left); Ethan Miller 63, 83 (above); Michael Ochs Archives 40; Redferns/Robert Knight Archive 68, 69; Redferns/Andrew Lepley 90; Redferns/Neil Lupin 61, 89; Redferns/David Redfern 41 (right), 66, 67; Redferns/Ebet Roberts 25 (left); Redferns/Steve Thorne 26, 60; Stone/Marissa Kaiser 11 (above); WireImage/Kevin Mazur Archive 64; WireImage/SGranitz 65; WireImage/Marty Temme 91.

Creative Commons License/public domain: alterna2 35 (below), 57; Matt Becker 89 (inset); Bertrand 86; chascar 71 (right); Compadre Edua'h 47 (right); daigooliva 48 (inset); dxburbuja 37; Rodrigo Della Fávera 36 (right); flimsical 82 (above); Italian TV 43 (below); JessicaSarahS 35 (above), 85; Ilias Katsouras 52; Anirudh Koul 75, 87 (right); Kreepin Deth 55; Kris Krug 33; livepict.com 44; Joshua Lowe Photo 54; Katerina Mezhekova 56, Malgorzata Milaszewska 59 (right); Kara Murphy 34; Scott Penner 19 (left), 84; SMN 32; Toglenn 74 (below); vazzz 43 (above).

Stonecastle Graphics: 16, 17, 22, 23 (left), 31, 38, 47 (left), 50, 51 (left), 62, 70, 72, 74 (above), 76, 78, 82 (below), 92.

Jacob "Quist" Quistgaard: 6.

© **Gibson Guitar Corp (press pictures):** 28 (left), 48, 88.

© **Orange Amps (press pictures):** 11 (below left and right).

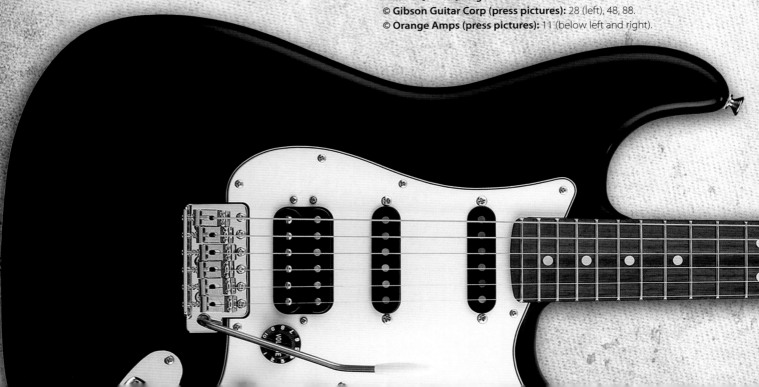

Contents

Introduction

CONGRATULATIONS ON taking a truly exciting step into the awesome world of Rock Guitar! You've chosen your instrument wisely: after all, it has caused revolutions in culture and style; and it makes hearts swoon, rocks crowds senseless, and keeps millions of people busy all over the world as they play, learn, and enjoy the magical thing that is music. Let's face it, the electric guitar is probably the coolest instrument known to mankind! Because it's so immediately accessible, it's popular across many, many musical genres, but has played an especially central, defining role within Rock, where it isn't just popular—more like *indispensable*!

Personally, I have been hooked on the guitar since I lifted my father's beat-up acoustic off the wall at the age of six. Playing has become a thing I love so much that I can hardly imagine not doing so every single day—I am totally and utterly addicted to those six strings! This book is the culmination of years and years of being the biggest guitar geek you can envisage: exploring the instrument; exploring music itself; jamming, performing, recording, and all the rest…and gathering a fair amount of experience in the process. I sincerely hope you will appreciate all the information awaiting you here. Please don't be afraid to *really* geek out and get deeply into the bits you love. Being a guitar geek is a win/win situation—after all, remember that you're playing the coolest instrument ever!

I've suggested listening references throughout the book. Enjoy them for what they are: examples that demonstrate how each specific scale, technique, and effect sound in real life. They will probably broaden your musical horizon, and have mainly been picked with that goal in mind—not as an attempt to express my personal taste, or to suggest that each selection somehow represents the "best" of what's being featured.

The following pages will get you started on *your* Rock Guitar adventure. They'll tell you about the guitar itself, about chords, about scales…and as you read on, you'll be able to study many—in fact, most—of the lead-playing techniques employed by the world's greatest guitarists. For that reason alone, you mustn't expect to be able to flick through the book, and master everything it contains in an instant. Instead, think of it as a big, beautiful mountain for you to climb. Some parts of it will be easy, some will test your patience, some you may want to put aside and return to later on—while other parts might even require additional help and support. But I really do hope you will have a lot of fun along the way.

Enjoy the book and the fantastic journey that lies ahead.

Quist

Opposite: This book's author, Quist, performing on stage.

This page: Some of rock guitar's major names in action onstage: Kerry King of Slayer (left), Slash (below left), and Muse's Matt Bellamy (below right).

Buying a Guitar

ANATOMY OF AN ELECTRIC GUITAR

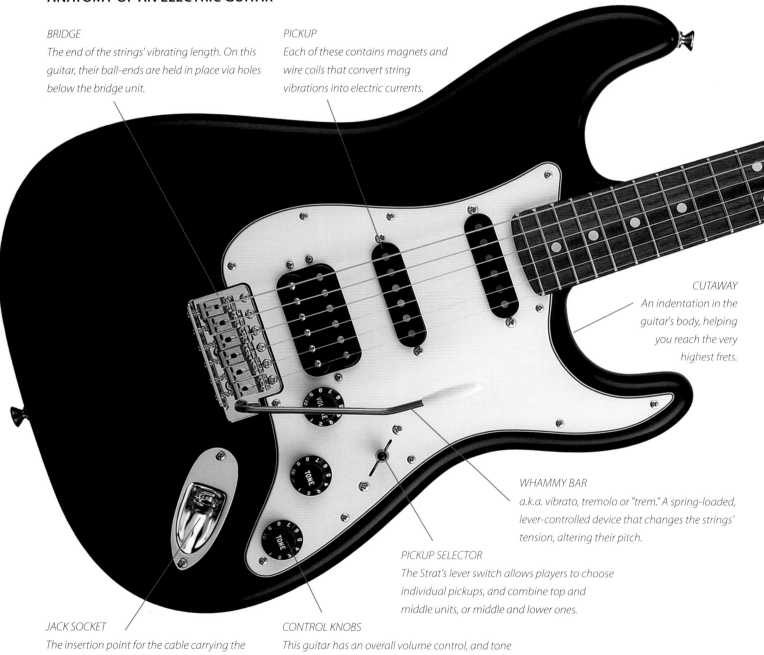

BRIDGE
The end of the strings' vibrating length. On this guitar, their ball-ends are held in place via holes below the bridge unit.

PICKUP
Each of these contains magnets and wire coils that convert string vibrations into electric currents.

CUTAWAY
An indentation in the guitar's body, helping you reach the very highest frets.

WHAMMY BAR
a.k.a. vibrato, tremolo or "trem." A spring-loaded, lever-controlled device that changes the strings' tension, altering their pitch.

PICKUP SELECTOR
The Strat's lever switch allows players to choose individual pickups, and combine top and middle units, or middle and lower ones.

JACK SOCKET
The insertion point for the cable carrying the pickups' signals to your amplifier.

CONTROL KNOBS
This guitar has an overall volume control, and tone knobs for the neck and middle pickups. The wider pickup nearest the bridge has no tone control.

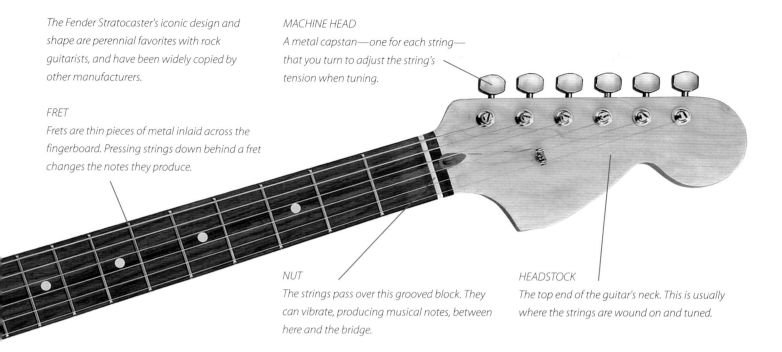

The Fender Stratocaster's iconic design and shape are perennial favorites with rock guitarists, and have been widely copied by other manufacturers.

MACHINE HEAD
A metal capstan—one for each string—that you turn to adjust the string's tension when tuning.

FRET
Frets are thin pieces of metal inlaid across the fingerboard. Pressing strings down behind a fret changes the notes they produce.

NUT
The strings pass over this grooved block. They can vibrate, producing musical notes, between here and the bridge.

HEADSTOCK
The top end of the guitar's neck. This is usually where the strings are wound on and tuned.

WALK INTO A music store, and you may be overwhelmed by the vast range of guitars on show. Here, we help you select one that's right for you. You're a budding rock guitarist, so you need an **electric guitar**, not an **acoustic** or **acoustic/electric**, which generally have round soundholes and deep bodies. Electrics come in several different forms: a handful of rockers favor **hollow-bodied** instruments with f-holes, but these tend to cause problems at very loud volumes, and you might not like their bulky look. Outwardly similar (though slimmer) are **semi-solids** like the Gibson ES-335, whose bodies have hollow internal chambers on either side of a central wooden block supporting their **pickups**. The block, invisible from the outside, helps sustain the notes produced by the strings, while the hollow sections add warmth to the tone—but you may feel that a semi-solid may not be quite right for you.

This leaves us with **solids**, like the Fender Stratocaster-style guitar in our picture. Their bodies are slabs of wood, contoured and shaped for style and comfort, whose density maximizes sustain. The downside is that most solids are quite heavy—so, when selecting one, be sure to check how it feels while sitting (with the instrument upright on your thigh) and standing (using a strong strap). Most solids have two pickups: the Stratocaster boasts three, but some players manage with only one.

We recommend that you go for a guitar with a **whammy bar**. The one fitted to our guitar is a good basic type, but for more extreme effects, you'll need a unit like the **Floyd Rose** system available on some Strats as well as many other solids; its locking **nut** helps to ensure that the strings stay in tune when using the whammy.

Above: The removable arm for the Stratocaster-style whammy bar screws into the right of the guitar's bridge unit.

Buying an Amp

ROCK MUSICIANS AND their audiences love loud music… and when playing onstage, guitarists in bands often favor very powerful amplifiers, combined with "walls" of loudspeaker cabinets. Their gear's visual "wow" factor can almost equal its ear-splitting decibel count—but because of its size and cost, it's utterly impractical for home use by beginners.

Another difference between "high-end" guitar amps and those designed for learning and practice is that the former tend to be driven by valves (vacuum tubes)—which have a pleasing warmth to their sound, but are fragile and expensive —while the latter rely on cheap, robust solid-state (transistor-based) circuitry. Transistors used to be spurned by serious electric guitarists, but nowadays it's easy to find an excellent, inexpensive solid-state amp, usually in the form of a "combo" containing both electronics and loudspeaker. One with an output of 15 watts RMS ("root mean square"—the standard way of measuring amp power) and an 8-inch (20-cm) loudspeaker should provide you with ample volume for playing at home. A built-in means of generating distortion, like the "dirty" channel on the amp shown opposite, is also a good idea.

Above: Whitesnake's Doug Aldrich with an impressive array of Marshall "stacks."

Left: When choosing an amp, it's worth taking time to ensure that it's well matched to your guitar, and capable of working in harmony with it to produce the musical results you are seeking.

Left: An electronic amp is designed to make the signal of an electric guitar louder so that it will produce sound through a loudspeaker. Guitar amplifiers also modify the instrument's tone by emphasizing or de-emphasizing certain frequencies and offering a range of different effects.

ANATOMY OF AN AMPLIFIER

The Orange "Rocker 30" combo: with its valve-driven circuitry and 30-watt RMS power output, this amp would be excellent for both practice and onstage work. It doesn't feature a headphone socket, but many smaller units are equipped with one—and the ability to mute the loudspeaker and play without disturbing others can be useful.

JACK SOCKET
The input for the lead carrying the signal from your guitar.

TONE CONTROLS
On this amp, only the "dirty" channel has tone controls. The three knobs allow the treble ("hi"), mid-range ("mid") and bass ("lo") response to be adjusted. The symbols above the "lo" and "hi" controls are, respectively, bass and treble clefs; these are used in musical notation.

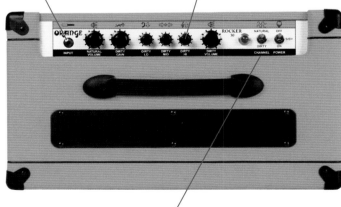

LOUDSPEAKER GRILLE
Behind the protective fabric covering the amp's front is a single speaker with a 12-inch (30.5-cm) diameter.

VOLUME AND GAIN CONTROLS
This amp has two channels, selected by the switch next to the on/off/standby control. The "natural" channel provides a relatively "clean" (undistorted) tone; the "dirty" one delivers just what it promises. By adjusting the gain knob, it's possible to produce lots of distortion even at a low volume setting.

Extras—and How to Tune Up

BEFORE GETTING DOWN to playing, you need to make a few more small purchases. The cheapest items are **picks** (a.k.a. **flatpicks**, **plectrums**). A few famous names, including **Mark Knopfler** and **Jeff Beck**, play with their bare fingertips and nails (**fingerstyle**), but most electric guitarists prefer the crisp attack they can obtain from striking the strings with a pick. Buy an assortment of picks in different shapes and thicknesses, try them out in turn as you practice, then select your favorite.

Our next three items aren't absolutely essential, but you'll be glad to have them.

A strap for your guitar

Though it's easier to play guitar sitting down, you'll often want to stand up when you're performing (or just posing!), so a strong, comfortable strap is very useful.

A stand

Guitars are easily damaged if they fall over after being propped against a wall or chair. A decent stand gives your "axe" the support it needs…and costs much less than a repair bill.

Above: A selection of different picks.

Opposite: Mark Knopfler is one of the most respected fingerstyle guitarists of modern rock.

Right: A good stand will help to protect your guitar from accidental damage.

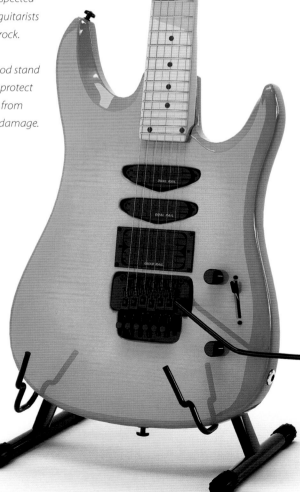

Above: A comfortable guitar strap will make playing easier and less tiring—even seasoned rockers like Motörhead's Phil Campbell and "Lemmy" Kilmister use them.

A case or protective "gig-bag"

Some guitars come with a free case or bag, but if you have to buy one, make sure it's rainproof, gives adequate protection, and has space for accessories. Don't put your guitar in a car boot unless it's in a hard case, and—at home or in transit—always keep it away from heat and damp.

Our last two items are vital:

Right: Electronic tuners are available in a wide variety of shapes and sizes, and make tuning your guitar an easy task.

A jack-to-jack cable

To connect your guitar and amp. It should be well insulated (so it doesn't pick up unwanted noise), and long enough to allow you to move around while you're playing. About ten feet is usually sufficient.

Something to tune your guitar to

Without a reliable reference, you can't set your guitar's strings to produce notes of the correct pitch. Some players tune their guitar to a piano, though this only works if the piano itself is in tune! Alternatively, you could use a pitch pipe or a tuning fork…but nowadays most guitarists prefer to use battery-powered **tuning meters**.

GETTING IN TUNE

Most electronic tuners have a jack socket you can plug your guitar into. Some of them are connected between guitar and amp, and allow you to tune up during a practice session or performance without having to replug your instrument. A few are "clip-on" devices that attach to the guitar's headstock; these measure vibrations from its strings without needing any input from the pickups. Connect up your tuner, following its instructions, and you'll be ready to get in tune.

Sit down with your guitar, hold your pick between the thumb and index finger of your right (picking) hand, strike a string (start with the thickest one: the **6th**), and look at your tuner's meter or LED display. It'll tell you whether the string's **sharp** (too high in pitch), **flat** (too low in pitch), or just right (**in tune**). If the string's sharp, slacken it off very slightly by turning its machine head, then check the pitch again. If it's flat, wind up the machine head—but again, only by a small amount before re-striking the string and seeing how your adjustment's changed the meter reading. Once you've sorted out the 6th string, follow the same procedure for the other five.

For reference, here are the note names and correct frequencies (in **Hertz** [Hz] or cycles per second) for your guitar's six strings:

STRING NUMBER	NOTE NAME	FREQUENCY
6	E	82.41 Hz
5	A	110 Hz
4	D	146.83 Hz
3	G	196 Hz
2	B	246.94 Hz
1	E	329.63 Hz

Some tuners can be set to different pitch "references." These relate to the number of Hertz used to generate the note **A** (specifically, the first A above "middle C," though you shouldn't need to worry about this!). The reference pitch for the A we're talking about should be **440 Hz**.

Reading Notation

MUSIC IS MADE up of **melodies**, **chords**, and **rhythm**, all of which can be written down very accurately using **standard notation** (a.k.a. "the dots"). Let's begin with an explanation of how the notes you've just tuned your strings to are shown on the five horizontal lines, and the spaces between them, that we call a **stave**.

At the start of each stave is a **clef** sign. The one used here is a **treble clef** or **G clef**: it curls around the stave's fourth line, and defines that line as a G—more precisely, the G produced by your guitar's unfretted (or **open**) third string.

Musicians name notes using the first seven letters of the alphabet in a recurring sequence; so once you know that the fourth line of the stave represents G, you can work out which notes the other lines and spaces correspond to. Here's the stave again, with note letters superimposed on it.

Our next piece of stave notation displays the note pitches for the guitar's four highest open strings: E (1st string), B (2nd string), G (3rd string) and D (4th string).

E (1st) B (2nd) G (3rd) D (4th)

What about the 5th and 6th strings (A and E)? These are lower in pitch, and won't fit onto the stave's normal lines and spaces. When writing them, we cheat by using **ledger lines** that extend the regular stave downward (or upward). Here are notes with ledger lines representing the two bass strings.

A (5th)   E (6th)

When notes appear in a vertical stack, like the E, B, and G (open 1st, 2nd, and 3rd strings) shown below, they're played together (strummed) as a chord, but if they're spaced horizontally, like the notes in diagrams 3 and 4 (left-hand column), they're sounded one after the other.

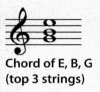

**Chord of E, B, G
(top 3 strings)**

RHYTHM

How do we show **rhythm**—the timing and length of our notes—on the stave?

Most music, and nearly all pop and rock, has a **beat**—a recurring rhythmical pattern you can tap your feet, dance, or move around to. Common patterns include those consisting of **two** or **four beats** like a march ("one-two;" "one-two-three-four") and a **three-beat**, waltz-type pattern ("one-two-three"). In all such patterns, the "one" is generally given a little more emphasis than the other beats.

TUNING WITHOUT CONFUSING

There's a confusing aspect to the way guitar notes are shown on the stave. If you asked a pianist to play the G written on the stave line that the treble clef curls around, he or she would strike a G **eight notes (an octave) above** the one you've tuned your 3rd string to. The pianist's note is correct—but guitar music is always written an octave higher than it actually sounds. You don't need to worry about this, except when tuning your instrument to a piano!

To write down rhythms on the stave, we use note shapes, with and without tails, that correspond to beats, fractions of beats, and multiples of them. The longest note normally seen in written music is what we Americans call a **whole note**, though elsewhere it's known as a **semibreve**. A succession of shorter note lengths fit into the semibreve/whole note as shown in the table below.

1 whole note or semibreve

= 2 half-notes or minims

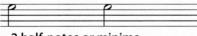

= 4 quarter-notes or crotchets

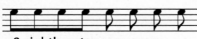

= 8 eighth-notes or quavers

= 16 sixteenth-notes or semiquavers

Quavers and semiquavers can be written with tails linked ("beamed") or separated. Beamed and unbeamed notes are shown here.

In musical notation, the recurring patterns of beats described earlier are organized into groupings that Americans call **measures** and Europeans call **bars**; and these are marked off on the stave by vertical lines called **barlines**. When a group of four **crotchets** (or **quarter-notes**) is being used, a **time signature** of 4/4 (four quarter-notes per bar—the "one-two-three-four" pattern) appears at the start of a piece's first stave. Other frequently encountered time signatures are **3/4** (a group of three quarter-notes per bar—the "one-two-three" pattern), and **2/4** (two quarter-notes per bar—the "one-two" pattern).

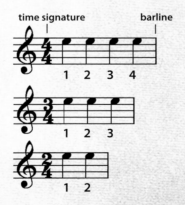

Note: In this book, for the sake of brevity, we have opted to use the terminology of minims, crotchets, quavers, etc, which is broadly recognized by musicians in both the U.S. and U.K.

Above left: Matt Bellamy, guitarist and lead vocalist of the alternative rock band Muse, performs on stage.

Above right: U2's talented guitarist The Edge uses rhythmic delay effects to create a distinctive chiming sound that has become a signature of the band's music.

Reading Tablature

STANDARD NOTATION provides lots of information about a piece of music—but figuring it out can sometimes be a distraction from the actual business of playing, and it doesn't tell you where to find notes and chords on your instrument's fingerboard and strings!

To make things easier, this book combines notation with a more guitar-friendly way of writing down music: **tablature**, which uses a set of six lines (marked "TAB") placed below the regular five-line stave. The tab lines represent the guitar's strings, with the 6th (low E) at the bottom; in fact, tab corresponds to your view of the fingerboard as you look down while playing. When you need to strike a note, a number appears on one of the lines. If it's a **zero (0)**, play the specified string open (unfretted). If it's a **1**, hold down the string behind the 1st fret; when it's a **2**, hold it down behind the 2nd fret… and so on. It's really that simple!

Tab indicates chords by "stacking up" numbers vertically. Our first tab chord is made up of open 1st, 2nd, and 3rd strings (E, B, and G); the only numbers in the stack are the **0**s on those top strings, so all the others stay silent.

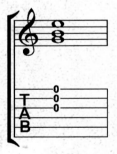

Next, you're being asked to strike the open 2nd, 3rd, and 4th strings, producing a chord (top to bottom) of B, G, and D. Again, the other, unmarked strings aren't played.

Now here's a bigger chord, involving all six strings. To play it, hold down the 4th and 5th at the 2nd fret (as indicated by the two 2s); tab doesn't specify which fingers to use, but try placing your second finger on the 5th string, and your third finger on the 4th string. The other strings are marked 0, so they're left open. Strum across all six strings once your left hand is in place.

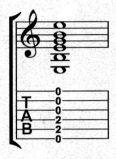

How was that? You've just played a chord of E minor! If you heard any buzzes or muffled notes, make sure you're holding down the 4th and 5th strings firmly, and not touching any others…then try again.

Above: *Fingering the E minor chord shown in the notation and tablature above.*

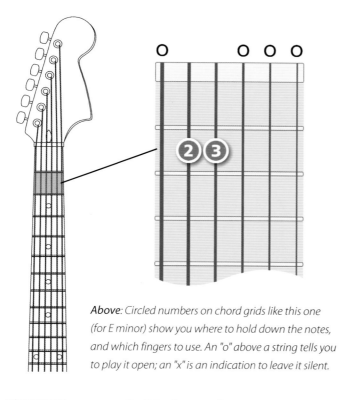

Above: Circled numbers on chord grids like this one (for E minor) show you where to hold down the notes, and which fingers to use. An "o" above a string tells you to play it open; an "x" is an indication to leave it silent.

Above: Moving from B flat to B natural on the fifth string—as in the notation and tab below right.

ACCIDENTALS WILL HAPPEN

Tab can often clarify potentially confusing aspects of "the dots." One of these involves **accidentals**—symbols that modify the pitch of regular, alphabetically named notes. The most common accidentals are the **sharp** (#), **flat** (♭), and **natural** (♮). When a sharp is placed in front of a note, it **raises** that note by a **semitone** (the smallest "official" pitch difference in Western music: each guitar fret changes the pitch of a string by this interval). You can see and hear two **sharpened** notes in the example below—the opening of the nursery rhyme *Frère Jacques*, played on your top string. By themselves, the notes on the stave would read E, F, G, and E; but here, we sharpen the F and G, and finger them one fret higher than usual.

The **flat** sign does the opposite of a sharp—**lowering** the pitch of a note by a semitone. And to cancel out a flat or sharp sign, we use the **natural**, which tells the player to forget about the previous accidental and play the specified note as normal. This little riff features a B♭ (on the 5th string at the first fret), followed immediately by a B natural (a normal B, played on the 5th string at the 2nd fret). Give it a try!

Accidentals only affect notes in the bar where they appear—so if we added another bar to this riff, and wanted to include a B flat, we'd have to use the flat symbol again.

RHYTHM PLAYING

Riffs

L ET'S START BY zooming in on one of the most important ingredients of Rock Guitar playing: the **riff**! This is a repeated melodic phrase or pattern—often simple, catchy, and memorable. A great riff can fill stadiums, encourage spontaneous air guitar-playing, attract screaming girls, and much, much more…but even though it may often be simple to play, coming up with one isn't all that easy. In the words of my esteemed fellow guitar-slinger John Wheatcroft: "A good riff is like a good joke. It encapsulates a musical idea in a very short space of time, and makes you think: 'I wish I'd thought of that.'" From Deep Purple's iconic "Smoke on the Water" to The White Stripes' pounding "Seven Nation Army," the riff is often the thing people remember best about the songs they love.

Awesome stuff…so let's tackle our first riff! Take a look at notation example A, below.

This is a simple two-note riff—consisting of an open E (6th string) and a G, played on the 3rd fret of the 6th string. The example lasts for two bars, with each bar consisting of four beats.

The first bar has four crotchets, which means you play a

note on each beat of the bar—open E (6th string) on beats 1 and 2, and then G at your 3rd fret on beats 3 and 4. I suggest using the second finger on your left hand for the G on the 3rd fret. You can play this bar with pick downstrokes.

In the second bar we start with four quavers, all played on the open E string again. This is followed by another G in beat 3, and a **rest** (see opposite above) on the 4th beat of the bar. Try playing this bar with "down-up-down-up-down" pick strokes.

Notice the double lines and dots at the start and end of the example. These are **repeat** signs, indicating that whatever lies between them should be repeated.

If you have trouble combining the notes and rhythms, try clapping the rhythms first. Also, practice the transition between the open E string and the G note slowly, making sure no unwanted notes are sounding, and muting the other five strings with your "spare" left-hand fingers if necessary. Here, your first finger will come in handy for this purpose.

Well done! Now let's play a four-bar riff, with a few more notes added, so take a look at notation example B, below.

This *rest* tells you not to play. The table opposite above contains rests corresponding to each note length.

Notes and Rests

semibreve	𝅝	𝄻
minim	𝅗𝅥	𝄼
crotchet	𝅘𝅥	𝄽
quaver	𝅘𝅥𝅮	𝄾
semiquaver	𝅘𝅥𝅯	𝄿

Right: Jack White.
Far right: Eric Clapton.

TRACKS FEATURING CLASSIC RIFFS

Kirk Hammett/James Hetfield (Metallica): "Master of Puppets"
—*Master of Puppets* (1986)

Jack White (The White Stripes): "Seven Nation Army"—
Elephant (2003)

Eric Clapton (Cream): "Sunshine of Your Love"—
Disraeli Gears (1967)

Keith Richards (The Rolling Stones): "(I Can't Get No)
Satisfaction" (single, 1965)

George Harrison (The Beatles): "Day Tripper" (single, 1965)

This example goes a little further, using principles that you could apply when making up a killer rock riff!

Bar 1 has four simple crotchets, two on the open E string, one on G, and then one on the open A string. Use your third finger for the G note throughout the example. Bar 2 has us playing four quavers on the cool-sounding B♭ (*see* page 17 for more about flats and other accidentals) on the 1st fret of the A string. Use your first finger. The rest of the bar comprises two crotchets, open A string and G. Then, in bar 3, we get two crotchets on the open E string, followed by a four-quaver phrase consisting of three F notes (on the 1st fret of the E string) and one open E to finish. The **root** note (E) and the F are a semitone apart (one fret)—and this is a very common move in hard rock and heavy metal. We finish with a whole bar of dramatic silence, allowing the music to "breathe" and imparting some nice suspense, before repeating the whole thing again.

Kirk Hammett

RIFFING

"My guitars are my umbilical cord. They're directly wired into my head."

Opposite and below: Kirk Hammett has been Metallica's lead guitarist for more than 25 years.

NOW LET'S HAVE a go at some real heavy rock riffing—in the style of Metallica's Kirk Hammett. Although it's possible to play this example with a clean tone, it works best with lots of distortion—so if you have a "dirty" or "drive" channel on your amp, switch it on!

The first thing we should talk about is **palm muting**, because this is an essential part of the sound. It's executed by leaning the palm (or rather the side of the palm) of your picking hand on the strings while you're picking, damping their sound by doing so. It works best with pick **downstrokes**, which we'll use for this entire example.

The first eight bars are focused mainly on the low E string. Fingering-wise, use first finger for any notes (on any string) at the 1st fret, second finger for the 2nd fret, and third finger for

Kirk Hammett was born in 1962, and grew up in El Sobrante, on the eastern side of San Francisco Bay. Like thousands of other budding players, he started out, aged about 15, with a cheap electric guitar purchased from a mail order catalog—but soon graduated to a Fender Stratocaster, and later to a Gibson Flying V. In 1980, he became a founder member of **Exodus**, a local thrash metal band; around this time, he was also having guitar lessons from rock virtuoso **Joe Satriani** (*see* pages 44–45). Exodus frequently supported more famous bands at live gigs: one of these was **Metallica**, whose members recruited Hammett in spring 1983 to replace **Dave Mustaine**. Hammett moved to New York to join his new colleagues, and his guitar work was quickly added to their debut album *Kill 'Em All*, released in July of that year.

Time pressure obliged Hammett to base many of his *Kill 'Em All* guitar parts on Mustaine's, but his own, strongly blues-influenced style—often featuring heavy use of wah-wah—is an essential part of Metallica's sound. His skills have been boosted by intensive periods of practice and study (he's been quoted as saying that he plays for 361 out of 365 days of the year!), and his personal musical tastes are remarkably wide; among his musical idols are **Alex Lifeson** of Canadian rockers **Rush**, as well as **Jeff Beck**, **Deep Purple**, and jazz saxophonist **John Coltrane**. Metallica themselves are currently rated the seventh biggest-selling band in U.S. history: their most commercially successful album to date is *Metallica* (a.k.a. *The Black Album*), released in 1991 and including classic Hammett riffs like the one for "Enter Sandman" (also a top-selling single). In 2009, Kirk and the rest of the band were inducted into America's **Rock and Roll Hall of Fame**.

Kirk Hammett is a long-time user of ESP guitars, and favors amplification by Mesa Boogie and Randall.

the 3rd fret throughout. The remaining eight bars are basically like a four-bar riff repeated, albeit with different endings. I suggest using first and second finger to fret the notes on the 7th and 8th frets of the A string. Beware of the rests five bars from the end: you'll need to silence the strings for all of beat 2 and half of beat 4 here, with the palm of your picking hand and/or your fretting hand. The notes at the 1st fret on the 5th and 6th strings in this bar are both played by the first finger. Don't "jump" from one to the other, try **barring**: placing the first finger across both frets, so the two notes are "set up" ready to be played, even though only one is sounded at a time. Rhythmically, this is the hardest bar to play, so take your time with it—clap the rhythm, and practice playing it really slowly at first. Rocking stuff, huh?!

Power Chords

OUR NEXT TOPIC is the **power chord**. You'll remember from Chapter 1 that chords are produced by sounding several notes simultaneously. Power chords are simple, but (as you'd expect) powerful, and are *the* most common type of chord in rock music. You can hear them in hard rock, heavy metal, punk, grunge, and many other varieties of rock. Fortunately, they aren't that hard to play—and lots of great songs rely on nothing but power chords!

At the heart of power chords are notes with a pitch distance (or **interval**) of a fifth between them. So every power chord contains two notes: the **root** (1st) and the **fifth** (5th). This is why they have names like A5, C5, etc., whose first part (the capital letter) tells you which note is the root.

Let's have a look at our first power chord now—and add some distortion if you can!

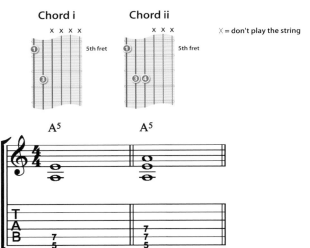

Chords "i" and "ii" here are both A power chords, also known as A5. In example "i", the **root** is the A note on the 5th fret of the bass E string, and the **fifth** is the E note on the 7th fret of the A string. The most common left-hand fingering for this is first finger on the 5th fret and third finger on the 7th fret. Use the rest of your first finger to touch the top four strings gently, thus muting them and ensuring that no unwanted notes are heard when you play this chord.

If you have trouble reaching between the frets, try repositioning your hand, moving the placement of your thumb as well, so the fingers become more aligned with the fretboard.

Above: Playing "chord ii"—the three-note A5 shape shown on the left.

Example "ii" is the same, but adds another A note, one **octave** higher. This doesn't change the name of the chord, as we're simply repeating the A (root) note at a higher pitch. I recommend using your little finger to hold down this top note at the 7th fret on the D string.

Now let's try moving the two-finger shape around and playing different power chords (see below).

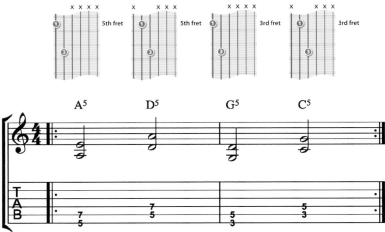

Using the very same fingering as the previous example, here we have four different power chords, played as minims—so each chord lasts for two beats. There are two with their root note on the 6th (E) string—and two with their root note on the 5th (A) string. For the latter two, you need to be extra careful with unwanted strings ringing or getting picked. Apart from being really precise about your right-hand picking, you could let the tip of your first finger lightly touch and mute the 6th string (in addition to "policing" the first three strings).

Above: The D5 chord in the notation at the bottom right of page 22, with the index finger "deadening" the 6th string.

POWER CHORDS IN ACTION

Kurt Cobain (Nirvana): "Lithium"—*Nevermind* (1991)

Josh Homme/Troy Van Leeuwen (Queens of the Stone Age): "Little Sister"—*Lullabies To Paralyze* (2005)

Billie Joe Armstrong (Green Day): "American Idiot"—*American Idiot* (2004)

Tom DeLonge (blink-182): "All the Small Things"—*Enema of the State* (1999)

Vigilante Carlstroem/Nicholaus Arson (The Hives): "Tick Tick Boom"—*The Black and White Album* (2007)

The final example (below) is testament to how easily you can move this shape around to create cool chord progressions.

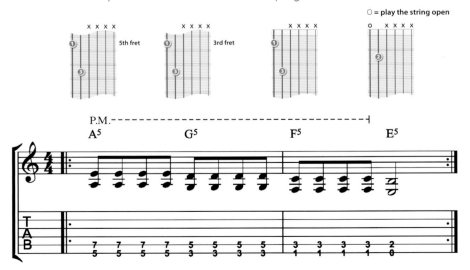

Above: Billy Joe Armstrong, lead guitarist for the American punk rock band Green Day.

Here we have three chords (A5, G5, and F5) each strummed four times, and one (E5) strummed once. Use your second (or first) finger to fret the E5. Also, add palm muting to the first three chords to get that awesome muted rock sound—and lift your right-hand palm off the strings for the E5 and let that one ring. Then repeat this two bar progression *ad libitum* and imagine playing it to a full stadium. *Enjoy!*

Kurt Cobain

POWER CHORDS

*"I'd rather be hated for who I am,
than loved for who I am not."*

NOW LET'S LEARN a chord progression in the style of Nirvana frontman and grunge icon Kurt Cobain. The piece uses three-finger power chords (with the added octave) throughout, so you are basically just moving the same shape around the whole time, the only exception being when you play the E5, which features an open E. I'd use my first finger to bar the 2nd fret of the 4th and 5th strings for that one.

The "A" section (first eight bars) is focused around playing two chord shapes per bar. Our main rhythmic pattern has the first chord on beat *one*, then a rest on beat *two*, and that same chord on *(two) and*. Then this rhythmic pattern is repeated for the next chord (sounding on beats *three* and *four and*). Use both hands to perform the rests: here, your picking hand should touch the strings to mute them completely, while your left-hand fingers stay on their notes/frets, but momentarily stop pressing them. Take your time practicing this maneuver, because those rests (on beats *two* and *four*) are one of the hardest things about this piece. You may also have difficulty moving between the chords fast enough to keep in time. Such trouble is very, very common, so practice each shift really slowly—and allow yourself to get used to moving between two chords at a time before moving on.

The last four bars combine palm-muted strumming of the G5 with a massive—un-muted—open E power chord. Rock on!

Kurt Cobain was born in 1967 at Hoquiam, a logging town on Grays Harbor in the northwestern American state of Washington; he grew up in Aberdeen, a few miles to the east. His musical tastes and skills were largely shaped by the region's rock scene, which was centered on Seattle, and spawned not just his own band, **Nirvana**, but also **Pearl Jam**, **Mudhoney**, and other icons of "grunge."

Cobain co-founded Nirvana with bassist **Krist Novoselic** in about 1986; its immediate inspiration was a local group, **The Melvins**, but Cobain's influences also took in **Led Zeppelin**, **Aerosmith**, and the **Sex Pistols**. Both **Dale Crover** of The Melvins and **Chad Channing** played drums for Nirvana (and are featured on its 1989 debut album, *Bleach*), but **Dave Grohl** replaced Channing in 1990, staying with the band for the rest of its all-too-short career.

Nirvana hit the big time in 1991 with the release of an anthemic single, "Smells Like Teen Spirit," driven by Cobain's distinctive guitar riffing; the album from which it was taken, *Nevermind*, became a multimillion seller, and is regarded as one of the defining records of its generation. The pressures resulting from such overwhelming success had a serious effect on Cobain; drug and health problems disrupted his work on subsequent material, and Nirvana's next CD, released in 1992, was a compilation disc, *Insecticide*. The group's final studio album, *In Utero*, appeared the following year, and proved to be another chart-topper. However, Cobain's personal difficulties had grown steadily worse, and on April 5, 1994, he apparently committed suicide at his home in Seattle. Nirvana's last live recording, an "Unplugged" session for MTV, had been taped in November 1993, and was issued on CD a year later.

Kurt Cobain's favorite guitars were Fender Jaguars and Mustangs, and he collaborated with Fender on the development of a new model combining aspects of both instruments. Appropriately named the *Jag-Stang*, it appeared in 1994, but at the time of writing is not in production. He used several different brands of amp, including Marshalls and Mesa Boogies.

More Riffing and Power Chords

NOW WE'RE GOING to dig a little deeper into the land of riffing, and start mixing single-note lines and power chords to create killer riffs with even more punch. From Black Sabbath to Megadeth, Rage Against the Machine and beyond, into the myriad of hard rock-derived styles that now exist, power chords and single-note lines have proved to be perennially powerful tools—and are still a vital source of awesome, memorable music.

Let's have a look at the first example (see notation A below), and once again, don't be shy—if you've got distortion, put it on and get ready to ROCK!

This is a repeated two-bar riff in the key of E minor, and combines the bass E string and a succession of power chords. Notice how two quavers on the low E string are played on *every other beat*—up until the last part of the riff, which provides a cool variation at the end of the cycle. This type of "call-and-response" structure is very common in repetitive riffs. All the power chords are best played using the standard fingering of first finger on the 6th string and third finger on the 5th string—and as mentioned earlier, remember you can adjust your hand/thumb position if you have trouble reaching the power chords—doing so can make your fingers feel much longer! Take your time with the moving power chords, and practice moving from one to the other quite slowly at first. That way, you'll help your brain to "code in" the correct way of doing it, and you'll be able to move power chords around real fast much sooner! I suggest playing the whole piece using downstrokes only—as this is very much within the style. And also, try it out both *with* the open E notes palm muted and *without*. Either way, it should come out pretty rocking!

Above: Black Sabbath founder member Tony Iommi. His Gibson SG's fret markers are mother-of-pearl "cross" inlays.

The next example (*see* notation B opposite above) comes from the even *heavier* side of rock—thrash metal and speed metal. This is the kind of riffing you could get from players like Slayer's Kerry King and Jeff Hanneman. (Slayer is one of heavy metal's "Big Four"—the other three being Metallica, Megadeth, and Anthrax). Take a deep breath and prepare for your arm to have a lactic-acid-build-up moment!

The main part of this riff is the rhythmic pattern on the low E string. It's played on the 1st, 3rd, and 4th semiquaver of each

A

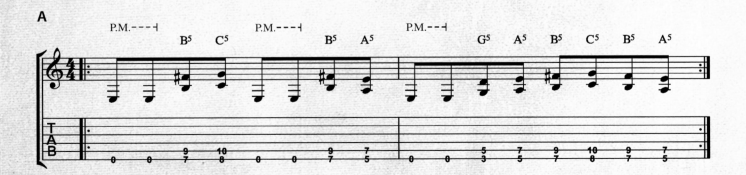

FURTHER LISTENING

Jimmy Page (Led Zeppelin): "Whole Lotta Love"—
Led Zeppelin II (1969)

Tony Iommi (Black Sabbath): "Iron Man"—*Paranoid* (1970)

Angus Young/Malcolm Young (AC/DC): "Back in Black"—
Back in Black (1980)

Kerry King/Jeff Hanneman (Slayer): "Raining Blood"—
Reign in Blood (1986)

Jamie Cook/Alex Turner (Arctic Monkeys): "Fake Tales of
San Francisco"—*Whatever People Say I Am, That's What
I'm Not* (2006)

beat. If you count each beat of semiquavers as "*one-e-and-a*,"
this means you are playing on "*one*," "*and*," and "*a*." The picking
pattern should be "*down-down-up*" for each three-note group.
Practice this pattern on the E string, before adding the power
chords. The next step is to introduce some palm muting, via
your picking hand as before. Then, when you're ready, add the
power chords at the end of the 2nd and 4th bars. Remember
to ease up on the palm muting for these chords, in order to
lend them some extra dramatic effect. Imagine playing whole
concerts full of riffs like this…it's hard enough keeping it going
at a reasonable speed for a few minutes!

*Above: Thrash metal band Slayer's Kerry King with
one of his strikingly shaped B.C. Rich solid-bodies.*

Jimmy Page

RIFFING AND POWER CHORDS

"I always believed in the music we did and that's why it was uncompromising."

Below: *Led Zeppelin's Jimmy Page: one of Rock Guitar's most flamboyant virtuosos.*

TO FINISH OUR journey through riffs and power chords, let's explore the style of riff-master extraordinaire Jimmy Page, who—together with the rest of Led Zeppelin—laid the amazing foundations for hard rock and heavy metal riffing back in the late 1960s. Before we start, switch over to your bridge pickup for a brighter, harder tone, and add a bit of distortion for good measure.

Our Page-style piece starts with a long phrase, best played with your third finger fretting notes at the 7th fret, second finger fretting at the 6th fret, and first finger dealing with notes at the 5th fret. Play the power chords with the usual fingering, except the open A5 chord, which only needs your first finger. You *can* play this piece with all downstrokes, but I suggest you try alternating between downstrokes and upstrokes in such a way that every note that falls on a *downbeat* (1, 2, 3, 4) is played with a downstroke—and those that fall on *upbeats* (1-*and*, 2-*and*, 3-*and*, 4-*and*) are played with upstrokes. This approach will work in your favor throughout the example.

The notes between bars 3 and 4 are connected with curved lines. These are **ties**, indicating that the linked notes should be played without a break—instead of actually striking the notes in bar 4, you just keep them ringing on for the duration of the tied note. Speaking of this…**dots** like those after the minims in bar 4 are an instruction to extend the duration of the dotted note by *half its original length*. So: the minim in bar 4 would normally be two beats long; with a dot, it's extended to 3 beats (2 + 1)…and the tied note in bars 3 and 4 lasts for a grand total of 7 beats (4 + 3).

The last four bars blend the A5 power chord with a bluesy, single-note line. Use your first finger to bar the 3rd and 4th strings at the 2nd fret for the A5—followed by second finger for the C at the 3rd fret of the 5th string. Then shift your hand slightly, and use first finger for the 1st fret, second for the 2nd fret, and third for the 3rd fret until the next power chord comes, after which the same happens again. It's basically a two-bar riff, which starts in two different ways. Cool. Now turn it up! And have fun rocking!

Left: A Gibson Jimmy Page Les Paul Custom, with gold-plated hardware and a Bigsby vibrato.

Jimmy Page was born in 1944 in west London. His family later moved to Epsom in Surrey, where Jimmy took up guitar at the age of about 12. He built a reputation on the local music scene, and went on to establish himself as a session player in London's recording studios. His work there was well-paid and varied (he appeared on discs by **The Who**, **The Kinks**, and a string of lesser names), but he found it uninspiring, and abandoned it to join **The Yardbirds** in 1966, playing bass with them at first; he went on to share guitar duties with **Jeff Beck** (*see* pages 80–81), and became the band's sole guitarist after Beck's departure.

The group broke up in 1968 with a series of Scandinavian tour dates already booked; for these shows, Page created a quartet known as "**The New Yardbirds**," comprising himself, singer **Robert Plant**, bassist **John Paul Jones**, and drummer **John Bonham**. Their decision to rename themselves **Led Zeppelin** was inspired by a comment, made some years before by The Who's **Keith Moon**, that another project featuring Page, Beck, and Moon would be as unlikely to take off as "a lead zeppelin."

Any doubts about Zeppelin's prospects quickly vanished. They attained massive fame during the 1970s, largely creating the genre of hard rock, selling millions of records, and grossing vast sums in fees and royalties. Stories of their offstage antics are now part of popular music mythology, but they ultimately owe their fame to their performing and composing skills—and particularly to Page's rich guitar style, a synthesis of rock, blues, folk, and much more. They disbanded in 1980, following Bonham's death, but the rapturous reception they received at their London reunion in 2007 (for which Bonham's son **Jason** played drums) demonstrates their enduring hold on their fans' loyalties, while Jimmy Page's post-Zep career—especially his collaborations, live, on TV, and on record, with Robert Plant—has also been artistically bold and rewarding. Page was awarded the Order of the British Empire in 2005 for his charity work on behalf of Brazilian children and the Action for Brazil's Children's Trust. He is closely associated with Gibson guitars, and has used amplification by Marshall, Fender, Orange, and many other companies.

Open Chords and the CAGED System

NOW LET'S venture a little further into the colorful world of chords. As you'll remember, the power chord only consists of *two* different notes—the **root** (1st) and the **fifth** (5th). Aside from power chords, the most common chords are **major chords**, which generally sound happy, and **minor chords**, which generally sound sad. Major chords consist of the 1st, 3rd, and 5th scale degrees, whereas minor chords consist of the 1st, **flattened** 3rd, and 5th degrees, though these notes can appear more than once within a chord. The first chords we'll learn are the basic and very common **open** chords—played in the *first* position and all involving open strings. I recommend sticking with a fairly clean sound for this section. Take a look at notation example A below.

Take your time learning these, because you can play literally thousands of famous songs with them! Try choosing two chords at a time, and practice switching between them very slowly.

The next step is mastering the **CAGED** system, which involves making the open chord shapes shown above into **"moveable" shapes**, or **bar chords**, with which you can play *any* chord in *any* key, as long as you're able to find its root (1st) note on your fretboard. Now look at the diagram at the top of the next column.

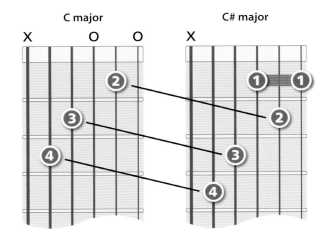

Take a C major chord, for example, and alter its fingerings as shown in this diagram, so that your fourth finger's now on the 3rd fret of the 5th string, your third finger on the 2nd fret of the 4th string and the second finger on the 1st fret of the 2nd string. All this frees up your first finger, enabling it to bar any number of strings…so now you can move your C shape up one fret (and one semitone) to C#, barring the 1st fret (only the three top strings needed) with your first finger. Nice!

Now let's have a go at playing one chord in all five shapes —which will take us up the neck! *See* notation B opposite above.

A

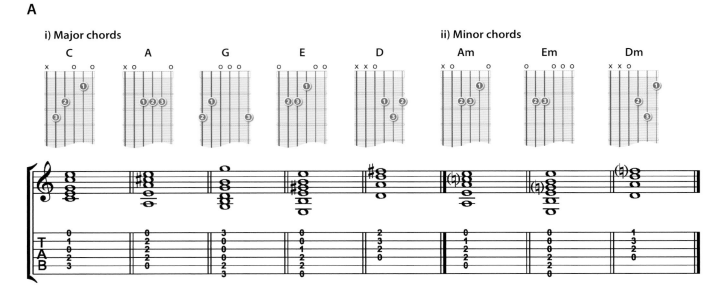

i) Major chords

C   A   G   E   D

ii) Minor chords

Am   Em   Dm

B

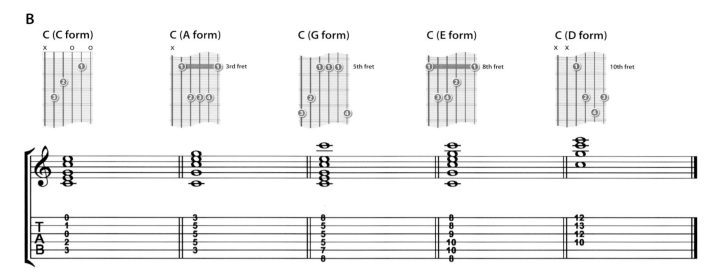

C (C form) C (A form) C (G form) C (E form) C (D form)

As you'll see from the example above, the CAGED system "travels" up the fretboard through the five shapes in a never-ending cycle. Let's focus for now on the "E" shape and the "A" shape, because these are the most common.

For this, we've picked a new root note—G—and we're exploring both the major and minor versions of the "E" (root note on the 6th string) and "A" (root note on the 5th string) moveable shapes. When playing these, using the fingerings shown in the diagrams, it's essential to make every note ring out clearly. See if you can play the chords without buzzes, one note at a time, starting from the lowest string. If you have trouble holding down the notes, try switching your hand/thumb position as mentioned earlier. And for the *minor* version of the "E" shape in particular, the 3rd string is sometimes hard to fret properly—I recommend "reinforcing" your first finger bar

with your second finger on top of that one, which appears as "Gm (E form)" in example C below.

Good luck!

Left: The "E form" G minor bar chord, with the first finger bar overlaid by the second finger.

C

i) Major chords   **ii) Minor chords**

G (E form)   G (A form)   Gm (E form)   Gm (A form)

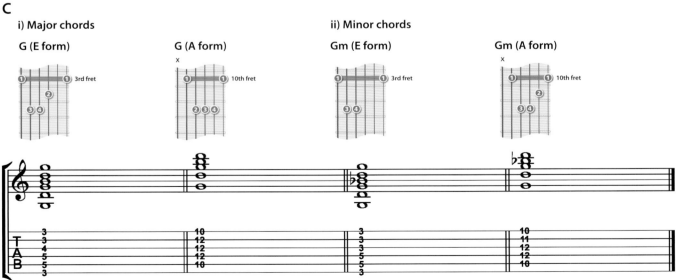

Jack White

OPEN CHORDS AND CAGED SYSTEM

"Music is what I have to do, I only answer the questions so that I can do it."

I F YOU WANT proof of how many great songs can be written with just a few open chords and maybe the occasional bar shape, look no further than one of the new millennium's most prolific guitar-playing songsmiths—Jack White. This White-style example (*see* opposite below) is based on the key of A, and its basic recurring progression of major chords (A, G, C, D) can be played with open fingerings only. The first repeated four bars can be played quite forcefully using all downstrokes. Use your palm to silence the strings for the rests—this also gives you time to move your fingers to the next chord. Line two (marked B) contains the same chords in two repeated two-bar sections: the first of these has us playing the root note and then "rolling" the pick across the rest of the chord tones, while the second one has a more vigorous strumming pattern.

Jack White's real surname is Gillis; he was born in Detroit, Michigan, in 1975. He started out playing drums, but switched to guitar when performing as part of a duo called **The Upholsterers**; he'd been an apprentice for the upholstery firm run by its other member, drummer **Brian Muldoon**. Gillis married **Meg White** in 1996: he took her surname, and formed **The White Stripes** with her a year later. Their subsequent divorce did not affect their musical partnership, and for some time they fooled the media into believing they were brother and sister.

The White Stripes (with Meg on drums) released their self-titled debut album in 1999, dedicating it to one of Jack's heroes, Mississippi Delta blues guitarist and singer **Son House** (1902–1988). While rooted in Detroit-style garage rock, White's music draws on a wide range of influences, and his eclectic tastes are reflected in his production work on albums by country music star **Loretta Lynn** (*Van Lear Rose*, 2004) and "The Queen of Rockabilly," **Wanda Jackson** (*The*

Party Ain't Over, 2011). The White Stripes brought him and Meg White international recognition: they first enjoyed major commercial success with their third CD, *White Blood Cells* (2001), featuring the hit single "Fell In Love With A Girl," while their fourth album *Elephant* (2003) won them two Grammys, and was their biggest seller. After six studio albums (the last was 2007's *Icky Thump*), The White Stripes disbanded in February 2011. In the preceding years, however, Jack White had been part of two other groups, **The Raconteurs** and **The Dead Weather** (playing drums with the latter outfit). He's recently been quoted as saying he won't join another band, and, at the time of writing, is working on a number of new musical ventures.

White frequently plays Gretsch guitars, but can also be seen with Valco "J.B. Hutto" solid-bodies produced in the 1960s for the Montgomery Ward mail-order catalog. He often uses Fender and Silvertone amplification, and his Digitech Whammy pedal is an important part of his sound.

Practice your strumming going *down-up-down-up* in semiquavers (*one-e-and-a, two-e-and-a*, etc.) before tackling the pattern in the last two bars of line B. The trick to playing this well is getting that "semiquaver" feel going, even though you're not actually hitting the strings on every semiquaver. Also, if you're finding it hard to switch between each chord, "open up" your grip on the last semiquaver of each chord and start moving your hand to the next chord. This results in open strings sounding, but that's perfectly within the style! The last three bars feature a big open E chord, and then bar chords for the rest of the piece. Notice how the "A" shape bar chords in the penultimate bar (E, C and D) leave out the top notes— that's quite common. Remember to slow down gradually (*ritardando—see* the notation below) during that bar, finishing by slowly dragging your pick across the A minor bar chord.

Left: In this close-up, Jack's about to play a downstroke.

Below: The "arrow" symbol that first appears in front of the second chord in section B is an instruction to "roll" the pick over the strings (see main text).

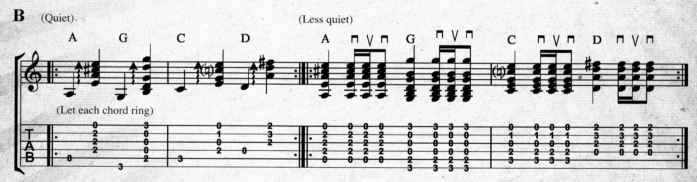

LEAD PLAYING

Three Scales

SCALES ARE THE patterns of notes we use to create tunes and build chords. There are thousands of scales out there —but a great starting point for rock guitarists is the **minor pentatonic scale**, from which you can quickly jump into the awesome world of lead guitar.

In addition to being one of the most commonly used scales in popular music, pentatonics are quite easy to play, as they contain only "five" notes (*pente* means five in Greek). So let's try one now—an A minor pentatonic scale starting on the 5th fret. Check out the notation and diagram below carefully to see exactly how it's done.

Your first (index) finger presses the 5th fret on respective strings throughout the scale; your third finger stays on the 7th fret, and your fourth finger on the 8th fret. First of all, play 5th fret on the 6th (lowest) string with your first finger. Then, on the same string, play 8th fret with your fourth finger. Move to the 5th string, play 5th fret with your first finger and 7th fret with your third finger. Get it? Continue all the way up to the top string—and then try going all the way back!

By including just one more note—which has the sinister nickname of "the devil's interval," because of its dissonant

sound—we can produce a **blues scale**. Go for it by starting from A as before, but adding a new fourth step to the sequence, supplied by your second finger at the 6th fret on the 5th string, and then, higher up, by your fourth finger (8th fret/3rd string).

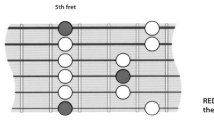

5th fret

RED dots indicate A, the scale's keynote

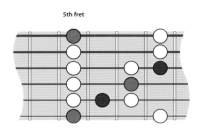

5th fret

Above: Dan Auerbach of The Black Keys at 2010's "South by Southwest" (SXSW) Festival in Austin, Texas.

BLUE dots indicate the "devil's interval" or "blue notes"

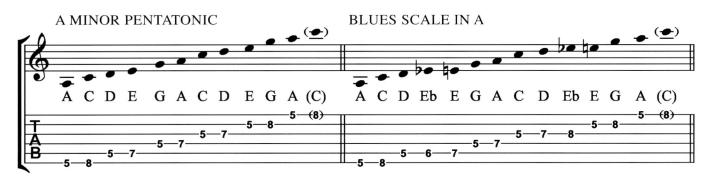

A MINOR PENTATONIC

A C D E G A C D E G A (C)

BLUES SCALE IN A

A C D Eb E G A C D Eb E G A (C)

Now let's focus on the **major scale**—the foundation upon which the whole of our music system is built. Here's one beginning and ending on A. Start with your second finger on the 5th fret of the lowest string, and follow the tab, notation, and diagram from there, using one finger per fret as before.

A MAJOR

A B C# D E F# G# A B C# D E F# G# A

SCALES IN ACTION

To hear how these scales sound in real musical contexts, check out the tracks listed below. For each of them, we list the featured guitarist, the band (in brackets), then the song title, the album from which it's taken, and its date of release.

MINOR PENTATONIC SCALE

Ritchie Blackmore (Deep Purple): "Smoke on the Water"—
Machine Head (1972)

David Gilmour (Pink Floyd): "Money"—*The Dark Side of the Moon* (1973)

Dan Auerbach (The Black Keys): "She's Long Gone"—
Brothers (2010)

Duane Allman (Boz Scaggs): "Loan Me a Dime"—
Boz Scaggs (1969)

MINOR PENTATONIC/BLUES SCALE

Tom Morello (Rage Against The Machine): "Bombtrack"—
Rage Against The Machine (1993)

Robert Fripp (King Crimson): "21st Century Schizoid Man"—
In the Court of the Crimson King (1969)

MAJOR SCALE

Brian May (Queen): "A Kind of Magic"—*A Kind of Magic* (1986)

Matthew Followill (Kings of Leon): "The Bucket"—
Aha Shake Heartbreak (2004)

John Petrucci

PICKING ACE

"I feel incredibly proud to be the type of band that we are."

HERE'S A Petrucci-style study that's a great warm-up and picking work-out, as well as a general finger coordination exercise. You'll want to use **alternate picking** when playing it. This means your picking hand always alternates between a **downstroke** (shown on the notation with ⊓) and an upstroke (∨ on the notation). Make sure you start with a downstroke when you play the first note—fretted by your first finger on the 5th fret of the 6th string. Then continue as indicated on the notation. At the start of bar 3, reach up to the 9th fret of the 3rd (G) string with your fourth finger, by making it "jump" from its previous position on the 8th fret, and continue back down from there.

⊓ = downstroke
∨ = upstroke

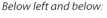

John Petrucci is one of today's most outstanding and original rock guitarists. Born in New York State in 1967, he enrolled, aged 18, at the prestigious Berklee College of Music in Boston, Massachusetts, where he and two fellow-students, drummer **Mike Portnoy** and bassist **John Myung**, formed **Majesty**. Its early repertoire embraced songs by Iron Maiden and Rush, and its name (which later had to be changed following objections from another group called Majesty) apparently stemmed from Portnoy's description of Rush's "Bastille Day" as "majestic." Rebranded as **Dream Theater**, the band released its debut CD, *When Dream and Day Unite*, in 1989, and Petrucci, Portnoy, and Myung remained at its core for 21 more years and nine further albums. The biggest-selling of these was 1992's *Images and Words* (one of whose tracks, "Pull Me Under," features in the video game *Guitar Hero: World Tour*). Portnoy announced his departure from Dream Theater in September 2010: it now continues without him.

John Petrucci's numerous side projects have included appearances on the first two **Liquid Tension Experiment** albums (1998 and 1999) with Portnoy and keyboardist **Jordan Rudess** (who subsequently joined Dream Theater); a string of appearances, since 2001, on **Joe Satriani's G3** guitar tour (Satriani performs with two other guitarists); and the solo album *Suspended Animation* (2005). His guitars are made by the Ernie Ball/Music Man company, and he uses Mesa Boogie amplification.

Another scale often used by John Petrucci is the natural minor (or, to give it its posh name, Aeolian mode). Let's try it out now.

Again, you'll be using "one-finger-per-fret" here…with a small exception when we reach the 3rd (G) string. Start by putting your first finger on the 5th fret of the bottom (6th) string, and continue with your third finger on the 7th fret and your fourth finger on the 8th fret. Then move on to the 5th and 4th strings, following the tablature.

Once you get to the 3rd string, you have to "jump" back one fret by placing your first finger on the **4th** fret, your second finger on the 5th fret, and finally your fourth finger on the 7th fret. Then you'll be ready to return to the original position, putting your first finger on the **5th** fret of the 2nd string, your second finger on the 6th fret, and so forth.

4th fret

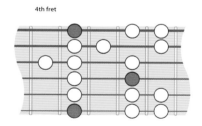

A NATURAL MINOR (AEOLIAN MODE)

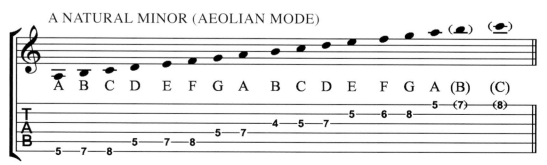

Legato, Hammer-ons, and Pull-offs

Legato

"Legato" is an Italian word meaning "bound together"—indicating that notes are played smoothly, with no intervening silence in the transition between one note and the next. In the world of Rock Guitar, the term is applied loosely, and covers not only **articulation** (i.e. how the notes should sound), but also the application of two specific techniques: the use of **hammer-ons** or **pull-offs**—instead of picking the strings—to play your chosen phrases. Most guitar virtuosi are masters of hammer-ons and pull-offs, and not only do they produce a cool sound…they instantly increase your ability to play fast runs. So let's get started!

Left: *Hammering on to C (the second note in the A minor pentatonic scale shown below) on the 6th string.*

Hammering on

A **hammer-on** ("h" in the notation) is performed by picking a note and then hammering down onto another fret on the same string—using your left hand only. Why don't you try and play the A minor pentatonic scale, which you already know (right), using hammer-ons?

Pulling off

A **pull-off** ("p" in the notation) is achieved by picking a note and then—without further right-hand effort, as before—"pulling off" the first note with enough force to make the second one ring. This may take a bit of practice. Again, let's try it out on the A minor pentatonic scale (below).

Right *Pulling off from 1st string C to A as the scale descends.*

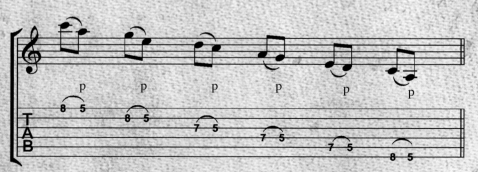

LEGATO IN ACTION

To hear these legato techniques being used in real musical contexts, check out the tracks listed below.

Jimi Hendrix Experience: "Machine Gun"—
  Band of Gypsys (1970)
Allan Holdsworth: "City Nights"—*Secrets* (1989)
Slash (Guns N' Roses): "Paradise City"—
  Appetite for Destruction (1987)
Mark Knopfler (Dire Straits): "Calling Elvis"—
  On Every Street (1991)

Now have a go at playing the scale all the way up—using hammer-ons—and all the way back down—using pull-offs. See how you're now picking only half as many notes with your right hand? Spot the potential for speed here? Basically, these two fundamental guitar techniques represent a cornerstone of Rock Guitar. So take your sweet time getting them under your skin—they are WELL worth the effort!

Next, check out these licks (below), which can be repeated over and over again. The first one uses hammer-ons; the second involves a pull-off on the 2nd (B) string; while the third one combines the two techniques—so here you'll actually play three notes in a row, having only picked *one* of them with your right hand!

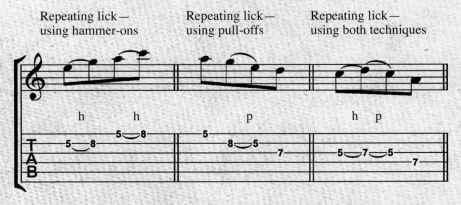

Repeating lick—
using hammer-ons

Repeating lick—
using pull-offs

Repeating lick—
using both techniques

Above: Slash displays his legato-playing skills with Guns N' Roses. His guitar is a Gibson Les Paul.

Have a go at making up some licks of your own, using hammer-ons and pull-offs on the A minor pentatonic scale.

Jimi Hendrix

HENDRIX-STYLE LEGATO

"All I'm gonna do is just go on and do what I feel."

NOW LET'S FOCUS on one of the pioneering wizards of electric guitar…Jimi Hendrix, whose extensive use of hammer-ons and pull-offs allowed him to achieve playing speeds *well* beyond most of his peers.

This Hendrix-style exercise is based on the A minor pentatonic scale you're already familiar with. Again, we play it with the "one-finger-per-fret" technique, using the first finger for any notes at the 5th fret, the third finger for notes at the 7th fret, and the fourth finger for notes at the 8th.

An important point when trying out this piece: even when they aren't holding notes down, keep your fingers directly above the strings and at the ready. If they're pointing in all directions while not in use, this will severely limit your capacity for speed!

Bars 5 to 7 of the exercise feature two notes played consecutively, over and over again. This is called a **trill**, and is shown in notation with the *tr*〰〰〰 symbol. To perform it like Hendrix would, you simply pick the first note—the 5th fret on the 3rd (G) string—then hammer-on to the 7th fret, immediately pull-off to the 5th, hammer-on to the 7th again, etc…repeating this pretty much as fast as you can for the full duration of the trill. Cool, huh?

The exercise's last line features something new—trilling between the 5th and 8th frets on your 2nd (B) string, and then pressing down on your whammy bar while keeping the trill going. *Voilà*—a classic Hendrix lick!

Check out Jimi's playing on "Voodoo Chile" from The Jimi Hendrix Experience album *Electric Ladyland* (1968): it's full of trills right from the get-go.

Jimi Hendrix was born in Seattle in 1942. He began playing guitar in high school: a left-hander, he used restrung right-hand instruments, turning their bodies upside down. After a spell in the U.S. Army (1961–1962), he worked as a backing musician for singers such as **Sam Cooke** and **Wilson Pickett**, but established his own group, the **Blue Flames**, in 1966. While appearing with them in New York, he attracted the attention of Englishman **Chas Chandler**, ex-bassist with **The Animals**, who became Hendrix's manager and brought him to London. There, he formed **The Jimi Hendrix Experience** with bass player **Noel Redding** and drummer **Mitch Mitchell**. Their debut album, *Are You Experienced?* (1967), took U.K. and U.S. audiences by storm, and Hendrix's performance at that year's Monterey Pop Festival was both musically and literally a fiery one…he concluded it by setting light to his guitar!

The Experience recorded two more albums: *Axis: Bold as Love* (1967); and the increasingly adventurous *Electric Ladyland* (1968), which included "Voodoo Child (Slight Return)," with its distinctive use of wah-wah. They broke up in June 1969, although two months later, Mitchell shared the stage with Hendrix during his Woodstock Festival set, with its epic, feedback-laden rendition of "The Star-Spangled Banner."

March 1970 saw the launch of the live album *Band of Gypsys*, with **Billy Cox** on bass and drummer **Buddy Miles**. The band split up before its release, and Cox and Mitchell partnered Hendrix on his final gigs. He died in London, aged just 27, on September 18, 1970, as a result of an overdose of barbiturates.

Hendrix's "trademark" guitar was a Fender Stratocaster, and he is closely associated with Marshall amplification.

Depress and release whammy bar

Depress and release whammy bar

The Slide

AS YOU CAN probably imagine, a **slide** is performed by playing one note and then sliding onto the next note, normally using the same finger. You can play a note and slide up to another, picking just the first one—**a legato slide**—or you can play a note and slide up, picking the one at the top when you get there: a **shift slide**. Let's try both now —using your first finger to slide with.

Play them both again, this time sliding down—from the 8th fret to the 5th—before moving on to the classic **long descending slide**. To listen to one of these bad boys, check out the very end of **Eddie Van Halen**'s monumental solo on **Michael Jackson**'s *Beat It*. Pretty impressive, huh? There's a reason it's considered to be one of the best Rock Guitar solos ever. If you have a distortion pedal or an overdrive channel on your amp, go ahead and turn it on: we want lots of "drive" for this one! Here we go—on the 6th string, sliding all the way down from the 17th fret.

LEGATO SLIDE
Slide up

SHIFT SLIDE
Slide up, also picking second note

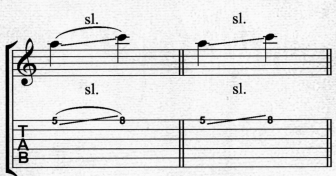

LONG DESCENDING SLIDE

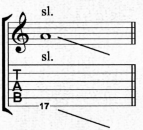

Below: Steve Vai performs a slide on his Ibanez guitar. His right hand is ready to use its whammy bar.

42

Try it out—slowly, and fast as well! Notice that you just keep going until there are no more frets to slide on. Of course, it would also be possible to land on a specific note down at the other end. Try coming to rest on a 5th fret A, thus sliding from A (17th fret) to A (5th fret)—all on the 6th string.

Now let's play our trusty A minor pentatonic scale using the slide technique, thus traveling out of its usual position and into new territory!

Right: Nuno Bettencourt of American rock band Extreme. Like many of his guitars, the one in this photo has a reverse headstock.

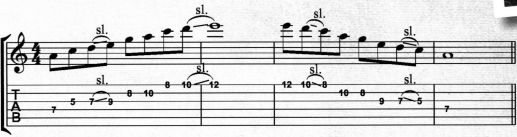

This example can be played using your first and third fingers only—sliding with your third finger when going up the scale, and with your first when going back down.

Finally, here's a cool lick combining legato slides and pull-offs. Repeat it over and over—slowly at first, then faster and faster as you get more comfortable with the moves and techniques in use.

Right: John Frusciante with an impressively well-worn pre-1965 Fender Stratocaster.

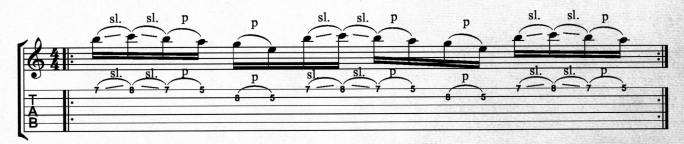

All these slides should be played with your third finger, and followed by a pull-off to your first finger. Notice how many notes you are playing, and how few of them are being picked by your right hand. I bet you're now beginning to see the potential for speed through legato!

SLIDING IN ACTION

To hear slides in use, check out these tracks.

Joe Satriani: "Summer Song"—*The Extremist* (1992)
Steve Vai: "For the Love of God"—*Passion and Warfare* (1990)
John Frusciante (Red Hot Chili Peppers): "Blood Sugar Sex Magik"—*Blood Sugar Sex Magik* (1991)
Nuno Bettencourt (Extreme): "Pornograffitti"—*Extreme II: Pornograffitti* (1990)

Now you're used to hammer-ons and pull-offs, we'll stop using "h" and "p" to notate them. Whenever you see notes on the same string linked by a slur like this [⌒], always play them with a hammer-on (when ascending) or a pull-off (descending).

Joe Satriani

EXTREME LEGATO

"When you hear something you don't like, don't ever play it again."

ET'S STEP UP our game another notch with an awesome phrase combining hammer-ons, pull-offs, *and* legato slides! This one is in the style of Joe Satriani, definitely one of the modern masters of legato on guitar. It's based on the A minor scale, but this time we move way out of the position we've already learned, in order to perform a cool sliding sequence that works its way horizontally down the neck.

Start on the 1st string at the 17th fret, with your third finger. Then use your first finger to play the 15th fret of the 2nd string—sliding down to the 13th with the same finger. In fact, with the exception of the 13th fret on the top string (where you hold down the note with your second finger), the first two bars can all be fingered with just your third and first, always sliding with the index. Give that a go now—and remember to try it really slowly at first, one little chunk at a time.

From the 3rd bar, it's all about this big legato lick on the 2nd string. Start on the 3rd fret using your first finger, hammer-on to the 5th fret with your third finger, pull-off to your first finger and then slide up to the 5th fret again with your first finger. Again, all the slides can be done with the first. Also, remember to stick to the "one-finger-per-fret" technique: you should use your first and third fingers when there are two frets between notes, and the first and second when only one fret separates them.

As you may have realized by now, the whole of the 3rd and 4th bars are played with a single, right-hand stroke! This is extreme legato territory, and you can hear examples of this kind of playing in lots of Satriani's music. Combining legato with lots of distortion works really well—and not only does it sound cool, it actually makes the phrase easier to execute!

Triplets
This exercise features groups of three quavers (eighth-notes) marked with a "3". These **triplets** are played by slightly "squeezing" the regular duration of each quaver, so that **three** of them (instead of two) fit into a crotchet (quarter-note) beat. To get the feel of how they work, count out the bar's four crotchet beats, and divide them into three: "*one*-two-three, *two*-two-three, *three*-two-three, *four*-two-three…"

Joe Satriani (b.1956) comes from Westbury, some 20 miles (32 km) east of New York City. He took up the guitar aged about 14 (influenced principally by **Jimi Hendrix**), and was skilled enough to start giving lessons to others barely two years later; among his early pupils was **Steve Vai** (*see* pages 68–69, 78–79). In his late teens, Satriani studied briefly with New York-based jazz guitarist **Billy Bauer** (1915–2005), and with Bauer's regular collaborator, pianist **Lenny Tristano**.

In 1978, "Satch" moved to Berkeley, across the bay from San Francisco, where he taught several soon-to-be-stars, including **Kirk Hammett** of **Metallica**, at a local guitar studio. His own band, **The Squares**, struggled for recognition, but his self-confessedly "bizarre" instrumental recordings—released as a five-track, self-titled vinyl disc in 1984—led to a groundswell of critical acclaim, and a contract with Relativity Records, which issued his first full-length solo album, *Not of This Earth*, in 1986.

Satriani's major breakthrough came with the platinum-selling *Surfing with the Alien* (1987), and in 1988 his profile was raised even further when he worked as guitarist for **Mick Jagger** on tours of Japan and Australasia. Satch's subsequent solo records have all enjoyed massive success —his biggest commercial triumph to date has been with *The Extremist* (1992).

His live work has included a stand-in stint with **Deep Purple** (following the departure of **Richie Blackmore** in November 1993), and he inaugurated the **G3** concert tours in 1996, starring in their initial line-up alongside **Eric Johnson** and **Steve Vai**. A string of other top guitarists has participated in later shows. Most recently, he's been involved in the rock "supergroup" **Chickenfoot**, with **Sammy Hagar**, bassist **Michael Anthony**, and **Red Hot Chili Peppers** drummer **Chad Smith**. His fourteenth studio album, *Black Swans and Wormhole Wizards*, appeared in 2010.

Satch has his own range of Ibanez guitars, and endorses Peavey amplification.

Scale Sequences

SCALE SEQUENCES may sound boring—but they really aren't! Not only will learning and practicing sequences hand you the keys to the Kingdom of Shred, it will also help develop your musicality, ears, general technique, dexterity…*and* give you lots to play with when improvising or creating solos.

So what is a scale sequence? Well, take our A major scale, which consists of seven different notes (the first and eighth are both As). Instead of playing it in the order of 1-2-3-4-5-6-7-(8), we can create a sequence by constantly "skipping" over a note—making the pattern 1-3, 2-4, 3-5, 4-6, etc. This could be referred to as "playing the scale in **thirds**" as the interval between these notes is called a third.

Note how the one-finger-per-fret system still works a treat on this new technique.

Here's a sequence for the A minor pentatonic scale, in which you go up in groups of **four** notes: 1-2-3-4, 2-3-4-5, 3-4-5-1, 4-5-1-2. Take your time and learn it slowly, picking every note. Then try it out with hammer-ons and pull-offs, as written. You need to choose a fingering that works for you and stick with it. For the 5th fret to 5th fret transitions, I would **bar** with my first (index) finger—lay the finger across both strings at once, as in the photo. For the 7th fret to 7th fret transitions, try using your fourth finger, followed by your third—or third followed by second. Reverse these fingerings when descending the sequence.

> The A major scale contains F#, C#, and G#. Here, those three sharps appear at the start of every line of notation as a **key signature**—an instruction always to play each indicated note as a sharp. Key signatures are more convenient than accidentals, and are frequently used for keys incorporating sharps or flats.

A MAJOR SCALE SEQUENCE IN THIRDS

A MINOR PENTATONIC SEQUENCE

Notice the added penultimate note, underneath the root A—to which you can slide up at the end.

Finally, let's play another popular *Rock Guitar* sequence, using hammer-ons and pull-offs. This one features the "triplet" rhythm you learned about on page 44, and we'll play it going downward in A minor pentatonic .

Don't forget to try out each of these sequences on *all* of the scales we've done so far! Then add another octave to the first example, working your way up the major scale. Also practice playing them using hammer-ons and pull-offs. The keys to the kingdom are now all yours. Have fun!

DESCENDING A MINOR PENTATONIC SEQUENCE

Left: Using a fifth-fret bar in the A minor pentatonic sequence shown opposite below.

SEQUENCES IN ACTION

There's no shortage of sequences in all kinds of music—but here are some great ones!

Slash (Guns N' Roses): "Sweet Child O' Mine"—
    Appetite for Destruction (1987)
Paul Gilbert: "Fuzz Universe"—*Fuzz Universe* (2010)
Dimebag Darrell (Pantera): "Cowboys From Hell"—
    Cowboys From Hell (1990)
Brian May (Queen): "I Want It All"—*The Miracle* (1989)

Above: Queen's Brian May with his self-built "Red Special" guitar.

Slash

SEQUENCES

"It's not so much how good a player you are, it's how cool you are."

Opposite: Slash's onstage garb inspires many imitators —there are even Slash-style Halloween costumes!

SLASH IS ONE of my favorite sequence users on guitar. In his world, sequences are not in use merely for the sake of playing long, fast, metronomic, and repetitive runs, but because it makes complete sense in the context of the music.

You'll often hear sequences in Slash's solos when things are building up to boiling point, but a lot of the time he'll only use snippets of sequences rather than one long continuous one, adding really interesting and varied contours to his phrases.

Our Slash-style sequence is in the key of E minor, so we'll be transferring our familiar scale patterns from A minor to E minor for this one.

Starting on the 12th fret of the 3rd (G) string with the first finger, keep two things in mind: maintain your "one-finger-per-fret" position for the first two bars—and use **alternate picking** for the two repeated notes in this

sequence, as restricting yourself to just downstrokes (or upstrokes) will severely limit your chances of attaining much speed. The second bar is a quick four-note lick, continuing the pull-offs of the first bar. Then for the third bar, we have the familiar "up in groups of four" sequence, but this time on the E minor scale, adding both pull-offs and slides. I'd do the first slide (14th–15th fret) with my third finger, continuing with the pull-off (15th–12th fret) using the same finger. The next two slides take us out of position: use third or fourth finger for the 15th–17th fret slide, and fourth finger for the 17th–19th one. On the last beat of bar 3, use first finger on the 15th and 14th frets (moving position), then fourth finger to reach the 17th fret on the 2nd (B) string, finally sliding from 15th to 17th fret using your second finger. Remember to practice this slowly.

Left: Gibson's "Appetite" Les Paul is based on the guitar Slash used for Guns N' Roses' 1987 album, Appetite for Destruction.

E minor always contains an F#, and this key signature tells you to play a sharpened F wherever it occurs.

Saul Hudson—better known as **Slash**—was born in London in 1965, but moved to the U.S. (his mother's birthplace; his father is British) aged 11. His childhood passion for BMX racing gave way to music after he acquired a guitar as a teenager. Already a **Led Zeppelin** and **Rolling Stones** fan, Slash became obsessed with playing, dropped out of high school, and, in 1983, formed the short-lived **Road Crew** in Los Angeles with bassist **Duff McKagan** and drummer **Steven Adler**. Slash and Adler subsequently joined **Hollywood Rose**, which split the following year. Its lead singer, **Axl Rose**, was formerly part of **L.A. Guns**—several of whose members came together with Hollywood Rose personnel as **Guns N' Roses** (the name explains itself!) in 1985.

After further changes, the "classic" G N' R line-up emerged: Rose, Slash, Adler, and guitarist **Izzy Stradlin** from Hollywood Rose, plus ex-Road Crew bassist McKagan. They recorded *Appetite for Destruction* (1987)—the biggest-selling debut album of all time—and *G N' R Lies* (1988). Adler's drug dependency led to his sacking in 1990: Slash, too, had serious substance-abuse problems, but underwent rehab, and remained with G N' R until 1996, although, a year earlier, disagreements with Rose had caused him to take time out and record the highly acclaimed *It's Five O'Clock Somewhere* with **Slash's Snakepit**.

Post-G N' R, Slash has devoted more time to session and guest appearances, working with **Michael Jackson** (who had already called on the guitarist's services for his 1991 album *Dangerous*), **Alice Cooper**, and other major names. He reconstituted Slash's Snakepit for *Ain't Life Grand* (2000) and a world tour supporting **AC/DC**, and has also enjoyed significant success with his most recent band **Velvet Revolver** (for which his long-time collaborator McKagan plays bass), and his solo album *Slash* (2010).

Slash plays a Gibson Les Paul, and is a devotee of Marshall amplification.

Bending

OUR NEXT TOPIC is bending—which, more than any other technique, will give your guitar sensitive, almost voice-like qualities. For this reason, we'll also be looking at adding **vibrato**.

To bend a string, you push it across the fingerboard, raising its pitch as a result. Usually, the string is bent upward, but it's also common to pull it downward, especially on the lower strings, as otherwise they'd be pushed off the fretboard! String bending uses muscles you probably won't have flexed before, and initially you'll probably find it quite an effort to change the pitch very much at all. But stay patient, practice regularly, and you'll soon be bending like the pros!

Let's start with a simple bend in the key of E minor.

A

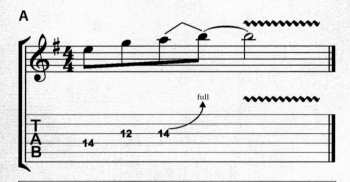

Note the angled lines in the notation indicating a **bend**, and the curved line with an arrow serving the same purpose in the tab. The "full" marking there tells you to bend upward by a **tone** (*see* right), and the "squiggle" above the last note is for **vibrato**.

Below: The 3rd string bend at the end of example A.

It's on the 3rd string, and is best performed with your third finger—the one most commonly used for bending. It's *essential* to line up your first finger (around the 12th fret) and your second finger (around the 13th fret) behind your third at the 14th fret: they should *all* be taking part in the bend to avoid strain. Also, use your first finger to make sure the 3rd string doesn't go underneath the other strings as it's bent. You're performing a "full" bend, which means raising the pitch by a whole tone (two semitones). You can check whether you're reaching the correct note by playing the 3rd string at the 16th fret—and then performing your full bend from the 14th fret. They should end up sounding the same. For the final part of the phrase, we just hold the bend. Once you're comfortable with this, try adding some **vibrato** by moving the string up and down, while staying centered on the original target note.

Now have a go at example B, shown below.

B

Again, we're using the third finger, supported by the index and middle—and this time, we're going to *release* the bend as well. After bending up a tone, let the string go back down to its normal alignment. You only need to pick the first note—the next one to strike is on the fourth quaver (3rd string, 12th fret). The following bar starts with a **grace note bend**. The grace note is shown in smaller print on the stave, and played at the 3rd string/14th fret. It's a little "decoration"—and you bend upward straight away as you pick it. Use your first finger to bar at the 12th fret for the next two notes, finishing with a pull-off on the B string.

Example C, shown below, features a **pre-bend**, for which you bend the string *before* picking it. As in previous examples, push up the 3rd string on the 14th fret, but don't let it sound until you've bent it all the way up to the B you'd normally obtain at the 16th fret. *Then* pick it—and release it as well. The next section features a regular bend, a pull-off, and finally another grace note bend: try playing this last one with your fourth finger, supported by the three other fingers. Give the final note a *wide* vibrato—shaking it up and down even harder than before!

Left: This photo shows how to finger the grace note bend at the end of example C.

Above: Joe Perry of Aerosmith executes a bend on a vintage, maple-topped Gibson Les Paul.

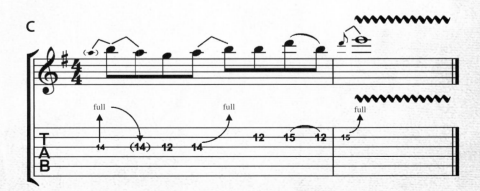

David Gilmour

BENDING

"I've developed the parts of my technique that are useful to me."

David Gilmour was born in the English city of Cambridge in 1944. He started playing guitar in his teens, and joined a local band, **Jokers Wild**, in 1962; three years later, they shared small-scale gigs with **The Pink Floyd Sound**—whose guitarist and singer, **Syd Barrett** (1946–2006), had studied alongside Gilmour at Cambridgeshire College of Arts and Technology. **Pink Floyd** (as they became) subsequently established themselves as the U.K.'s top psychedelic group, but their success took a heavy toll on Barrett's mental health, and in early 1968 Gilmour, who had been busking in Europe following the break-up of Jokers Wild, was brought in to replace him. His first recordings with Floyd appeared on their second album, *A Saucerful of Secrets* (1968).

Gilmour's distinctive electric and acoustic guitar work soon made its mark, and some of his finest playing can be heard on Pink Floyd's *Meddle* (1971), and *Dark Side of the Moon* (1973)—currently ranked third in the list of all-time worldwide best-sellers. He released a solo album, *David Gilmour*, in 1978, a year before the launch of Floyd's epic, *The Wall*. Musical and personal tensions within the band led him to undertake numerous side projects over the next few years, including another solo record (*About Face*, 1984), and coproduction of **The Dream Academy's** debut album in 1985. He took artistic charge of Pink Floyd after bassist **Roger Waters'** departure in 1986, though the band was briefly reunited for the Live 8 concert at London's Earl's Court on July 2, 2005.

David Gilmour's most recent albums are *On An Island* (2006) and *Live in Gdańsk* (2008), and in 2004 he starred, with other members of "**The Strat Pack**," at a Wembley Stadium show marking half a century of the Fender Stratocaster. A long-time Fender player, he is also famous for his use of amplifiers by British manufacturer Hiwatt.

FOR ANYONE aspiring to solo with lots of feeling, I recommend checking out the work of Pink Floyd's David Gilmour. An absolute master of the bending technique, he uses it to great effect in many of his solos—such as the classic Pink Floyd track "Another Brick in the Wall, Part II."

We stay in the key of E Minor for the David Gilmour-style bending example shown here (*see* opposite). Starting out with a simple bend, play the next two notes using your first finger to bar the top two strings at the 12th fret. The following three 3-note phrases constitute a **sequence**. The first and third of them each contain a pull-off, while the second one features the familiar "pre-bend and release" combination. In bar 3, we have a long sustained grace note bend with added vibrato—and Gilmour's trademark **multiple bend** technique in bar 4. Use either your third or fourth finger for these bends. For the multiple bend, you bend up a whole tone from the 15th fret (to

the equivalent sound you'd obtain at the 17th fret). Then, as you're holding the bend, push it up *another* whole tone—a full two tones above the original note (equaling the sound at the 19th fret). Now, gradually release down to the 15th fret, finishing by simply picking the same note and adding vibrato. In bars 7, 8, and 9, we move out of the original position. Use

your third finger for the 17th fret bend, and first finger on the 15th fret. The bend in bar 9 can be performed with just the first finger (no other fingers helping out). Revert to the original position after this, concluding the final phrase with another vibrato-infused bend. These techniques require considerable strength, and may take time to perfect.

Arpeggios

OUR NEXT TOPIC is the **arpeggio**—which is just a fancy (well, *Italian*) word for playing the notes of a chord one at a time. To construct a major or minor chord, you take the 1st, 3rd, and 5th note from its scale. If you play the notes all together at the same time, you get a **chord**. And by playing them one by one, you get an **arpeggio**. Simple!

So let's have a look at a C major arpeggio.

As you can see, we play the 1st note from the scale (C), the 3rd (E), and the 5th (G)—starting at C on the 8th fret of the low E string, and ending at C on the 8th fret of the high E string, two octaves above.

Rock guitarists often use **sweep picking** when playing arpeggios. Sweep picking basically means continuing a downstroke or upstroke whenever possible, allowing you to sweep smoothly and *quickly* (!) across the strings. Check out Frank Gambale: he's arguably one of the best sweep pickers in the world.

Fingering is paramount when playing arpeggios, especially when sweep picking, because there's no gain in being able to pick fast with your right hand if your left hand can't match up. For the notation above, I suggest using fingers 2, 1, 3, 4, 2, 1, and 1. Alternatively, try a bar (with either your third or fourth finger) between the A (5th) string and the D (4th) string. Go backward as well, using the same fingering in reverse.

Now let's play an arpeggio pattern that's even easier to "sweep pick"…

Here, I'd use fingers 3, 2, 1, 1, and 4—and the same going back. Notice how the pull-off on the high E string allows you to play the pattern using *one* downward sweep and *one* upward one. Practice slowly, and repeat over and over until you can play it steadily, with each note ringing clearly.

For the last example, we have two different C minor arpeggio shapes (*see* example below). Again, we'll use the sweep/pull-off combination. Check out Kirk Hammett's work with Metallica for more examples of this.

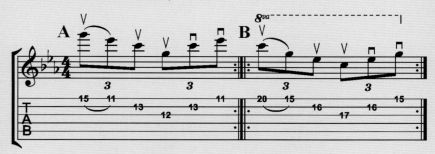

For arpeggio pattern A, I'd finger 4, 1, 3, 2—going back up using the same fingers. For pattern B, I'd use 4, 1, 2, 3—again using the same fingers to return. Remember to take your time with this—sweep picking takes a while to perfect. You have to practice it *painfully* slowly, allowing yourself to get into the habit of playing it right every time, and keeping the execution nice and precise.

ARPEGGIOS IN ACTION

Yngwie Malmsteen: "Demon Driver"—*Eclipse* (1990)
Synyster Gates (Avenged Sevenfold): "Afterlife"—
   Avenged Sevenfold (2007)
Frank Gambale: "Leave Ozone Alone"—
   Thunder from Down Under (1990)
Kirk Hammett (Metallica): "Leper Messiah"—
   Master of Puppets (1986)

Left: Synyster Gates of Avenged Sevenfold (A7X for short). His guitar is a Schecter.

Above right: Kirk Hammett fires off an arpeggio.

C MINOR & "8*va*"

Our last musical example on these pages is in *C minor* (*see* below), which has a key signature you won't have seen before. It contains three flats—B♭, A♭, and E♭—though quite often music written in C minor "cancels" the flats on A♭ (the sixth step of the scale) and B♭ (the seventh step) with an **accidental** natural symbol (♮), placed in front of a specific note, and only applying within the bar where it appears.

There's another new symbol here: the **8*va*** indication (with its associated dotted line) above the six notes of arpeggio pattern B in our final example. This tells you to play the marked notes an **octave** (eight notes) higher than they're written. It's used in order to avoid having to place notes above the stave with lots of ledger lines—and doesn't affect the tab, which, as always, shows you the correct fret positions for fingering these high notes.

These notes.............actually sound as.........

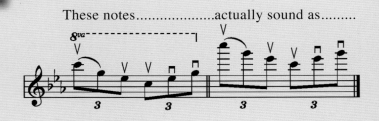

55

Yngwie Malmsteen

ARPEGGIOS

NOW LET'S CHECK out someone who features loads of arpeggios in his music: neo-classical Rock Guitar virtuoso Yngwie Malmsteen. Yngwie was originally inspired by composers like Bach and Paganini, and this is especially apparent in his use of arpeggios.

Our example, inspired by Yngwie's playing, is in C minor. However, in true Yngwie style, it includes the C **harmonic** minor scale, and also displays some very "classical-sounding" **diminished** arpeggios made up of a succession of **minor thirds**—intervals of three semitones. Start on a downstroke or an upstroke: it's up to you, and both are shown on the notation. A great fingering for the first bar would be 4, 1, 1, 1 for the C minor arpeggio (for convenience and clarity, the names of the chords from which the arpeggios are formed appear above the stave), and 4, 1, 2, 1 for the B♭ one. There are very rapid position shifts throughout, so make sure you practice each arpeggio very slowly, getting it right every time before you move on to the next.

For the next bar, I'd use fingers 4, 1, 3, 2 for the C minor arpeggio, and then either 4, 1, 3 or 3, 1, 2 for the following two diminished arpeggio patterns. For the third bar, use 4, 1, 2, 3 on the C minor arpeggio, and 4, 1, 1, 2 on the G major arpeggio. The last C minor arpeggio can be played with one long upstroke, using a single downstroke for the last note. Fingering-wise, I would go for 4, 1, 2, 3, 3, 4, 1. Alternatively, try out 4, 1, 2, 3, 2, 3, 1—or a combination of the two. Have fun with this!

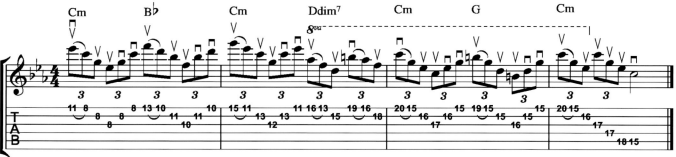

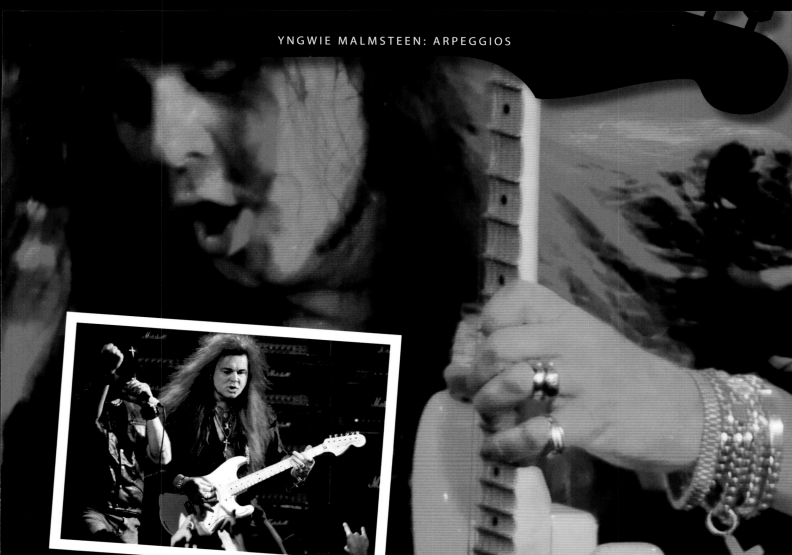

The ultra-high-speed playing style known as **shredding** owes much of its popularity to Sweden's **Yngwie Malmsteen**—an innovative influence on this genre for more than two decades, and an artist who draws inspiration from both rock music and classical virtuosi, such as violinist **Niccolò Paganini** (1782–1840). Yngwie was born in Stockholm in 1963, and claims that his passion for electric guitar was triggered when, as a seven-year-old, he watched coverage of **Jimi Hendrix's** death on TV. Like Hendrix, and another early influence, **Ritchie Blackmore** of **Deep Purple**, he has always favored Fender Stratocasters and Marshall amplification, and was already using this gear when he came to the U.S. in 1982, seeking to make his name there.

His first high-profile American project was a contribution to **Steeler**'s self-titled 1983 album, replacing the band's original lead guitarist, **Michael Dunigan**. However, he soon moved on to membership of **Alcatrazz**, before striking out on his own with **Rising Force**—the

name he used as the title of his debut solo album, released in 1984, and subsequently adopted for his band. They went on to enjoy massive success live and on disc: their shows included gigs in the Soviet Union during 1989 (two years before its dissolution), recordings of which appeared on CD as *Live in Leningrad: Trial By Fire*.

Away from Rising Force, Yngwie Malmsteen's most unusual venture has been the composition and performance of his *Concerto Suite for Electric Guitar and Orchestra*, first recorded in 1998 with the Czech Philharmonic, and later issued in a live version with the New Japan Philharmonic (2001). His work has always been highly regarded in Asia and Europe, and though his fortunes have sometimes fluctuated in the United States, American audiences have recently regained their enthusiasm for his unique approach—as is shown by the acclaim with which his albums *Perpetual Flame* (2009) and *Relentless* (2010) have been received.

String Skipping

OUR NEXT TOPIC is **string skipping**, which—as the name suggests—is simply about skipping strings when playing. This technique is very effective for playing wider intervals, and when you start mixing it with hammer-ons, pull-offs, slides, and so on, you can come up with some seriously cool licks!

Let's give it a go on the C minor pentatonic scale.

Starting on the 8th fret, you play the usual two scale notes on the 6th string, and then—skipping the 5th string—you play the next two scale notes on the 4th string. Now move to the 5th string, skipping on to the 3rd string. You see the pattern? This is actually a sequence, as we stick with it all the way. Play it, picking every note at first. Then try using hammer-ons as written. Make sure you use alternate picking in both cases—practicing really slowly, as your right hand will need time to get used to the skipping between the strings. Don't despair if you keep picking the wrong strings, or can't seem to find the string with your picking hand—it takes a while to acquire the necessary precision! Remember, the slower you practice, the faster you'll learn it.

TRACKS FEATURING STRING SKIPPING

Paul Gilbert: "Olympic"—*Fuzz Universe* (2010)
Eric Johnson: "Cliffs of Dover"—*Ah Via Musicom* (1990)
John Scofield: "Whip The Mule"—*Hand Jive* (1994)
Chris Broderick (Megadeth): "44 Minutes"— *Endgame* (2009)

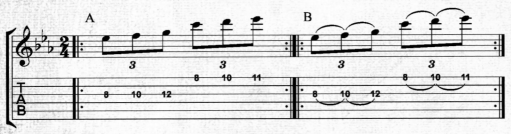

Right: Eric Johnson skipping strings at a gig, with his whammy bar in easy reach of his picking hand.

Opposite: Another skilled exponent of this technique: Megadeth's Chris Broderick.

It's very common to use three-notes-per-string patterns when string skipping. At the bottom of page 58, there's one on a C minor scale that you can practice repeatedly, gradually building up your speed. Again, use alternate picking—both for version **A**, where every note is picked, and for version **B**, where hammer-ons are used. I suggest using fingers 1, 2, and 4 on the 3rd string, and 1, 2, and 3 on the 1st string.

The final example (below) prepares us for the next section, where we'll explore the work of a master of string skipping. It's a C major arpeggio.

This is basically a clever, alternative way to play arpeggios. By adding legato to the mix, you obtain a completely different sound and phrasing than you'd get with basic picking or sweep picking. Fingering-wise, use the second finger on the 4th string, and first and fourth on the 3rd string as well as the 1st string. Take your time with this, it's not easy—but once you've gotten used to both the swift moves and the legato combinations this technique really does open the door to a whole new world of opportunities.

Paul Gilbert

STRING SKIPPING

"To learn to play guitar, you have to spend a lot of time by yourself with the instrument."

IN TERMS OF applying the string-skipping technique, few do it as much *and* as effectively as virtuoso rock guitarist Paul Gilbert. In particular, Paul has found a great way of using string skipping and legato to play arpeggios. We looked briefly at this technique on the last two pages, and here we're exploring it in more depth—using minor and major arpeggios, and switching swiftly with our fingers between different positions on the fretboard.

We'll stay with C as our root for this one.

The first bar contains a C minor arpeggio, starting at the 11th fret on the 1st string, pulling off to the 8th fret. You then play 12th fret on the 3rd string, pulling off to the 8th fret—and proceeding to the 10th fret on the 4th string. After that you go back up, obviously using a hammer-on, rather than pull-offs. This same procedure continues throughout the next three bars, though these feature **major** arpeggios (G, B♭, F), and different string sets (in bars 2 and 4). The 5th bar contains a C major arpeggio, with a slightly elaborated pattern. We finish on the root in bar 6, adding a touch of vibrato to the last note as it rings. Phew!

These are my suggested fingerings for each arpeggio:

Cm = 3, 1, 4, 1, 2 (1, 4, 1) / G = 4, 1, 4, 1, 2 (1, 4, 1)
B♭ = 4, 1, 4, 1, 2 (1, 4, 1) / F = 4, 1, 4, 1, 2 (1, 4, 1)

For the C major arpeggio lick in the 5th bar, the fingering is 4, 1, 2, 1, 4, 1, 4, 1—ending with your second finger on the 10th fret of the 4th string in bar 6.

Remember to practice this example *extremely* slowly at first —playing one arpeggio at a time before going on to switch between two arpeggios, three arpeggios, etc. Breaking it down is the most efficient way of learning hard stuff quickly!

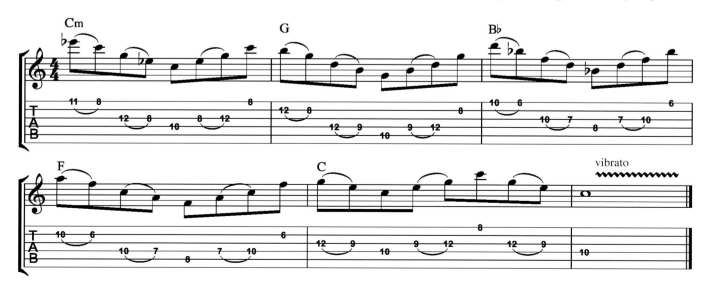

Many league tables of outstandingly fast rock guitarists feature American shredder **Paul Gilbert** in their "top five" —often in close proximity to one of his principal influences, **Yngwie Malmsteen** (*see* pages 56–57). Gilbert is some three years younger than the Swedish maestro: born in Illinois in 1966, he had developed an awesomely powerful technique by the time he was a teenager…though even he wasn't able to realize his ambition of working with **Ozzy Osbourne's** band at that age! Gilbert got his big break in 1985, when, after finishing his studies at Los Angeles' prestigious **Guitar Institute of Technology** (and while still teaching there), he became a founder member of one of LA's hottest young groups, **Racer X**. During his first three-year stint with them, they made two studio albums—*Street Lethal* (1986) and *Second Heat* (1987)—plus a pair of live CDs, both entitled *Extreme Volume*. The first of these was released in 1988, the year Gilbert quit the band; its successor didn't appear for another four years.

Gilbert's next group, **Mr. Big**, enjoyed massive acclaim, and a worldwide hit single (*To Be With You*, taken from the band's 1991 album *Lean Into It*). He stayed with them until 1997, then launched his solo career with *King of Clubs* (1998), and combined it with a rich variety of side projects— including **Hammer of the Gods** (a group formed to pay homage to **Led Zeppelin**), and a guest appearance on 2007's **G3** tour. He is also part of reformed line-ups of Racer X and Mr. Big, both of which have toured and recorded extensively in recent years.

Japanese guitar manufacturer Ibanez has produced PGMs (Paul Gilbert Models—some with painted-on *trompe l'oeil* f-holes) since 1989, and Paul currently favors Marshall amplification.

Tapping

NOW LET'S LOOK at one of the flashiest of all electric guitar techniques—**tapping**. Eddie Van Halen (*see pages 64–65*) played a huge part in bringing it into the mainstream, and since then it's developed immensely. Search the videos on *YouTube* to discover how tapping's currently being used in all manner of fantastic ways…from two-handed tapping, with literally every finger on both hands in use, to lightning-speed trills where the **pick** is used to tap the fretboard instead of the finger.

Tapping basically means using your picking hand to "tap" the string against the fretboard—usually with the middle or index finger. Very often, pull-offs and hammer-ons are also incorporated, combining right hand and left hand, and enabling you to create very fast legato phrases with relative ease. Sound like fun? You bet! Let's give it a go.

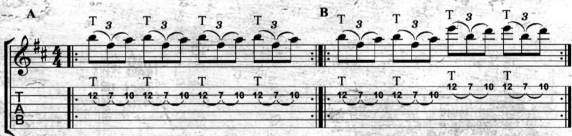

Above: The first "tap" in our first example opposite sounds a B on the 2nd string.

At the start of our first example, on a B minor pentatonic scale, you "hammer" down on the 12th fret of the 2nd string—where "T" for "tap" appears in the notation—using either the index or middle finger of your picking hand. Next comes a pull-off to the 7th fret with your tapping finger. Practice this move *loads* before moving on. Then add the 7th-to-10th fret

hammer-on. I'd go for first finger on the 7th fret, and fourth on the 10th fret. Now repeat that three-note lick. Practice it really slowly, keeping the triplets steady, and sounding each note as strongly as the previous one. Then try out example B. Here, you play the same pattern on the E string as well, and alternate between the two strings. Repeat exercises "A" and "B" several times—and expect a sore fingertip on your tapping hand!

Count 4 - and - 1 - and - 2 - and - (etc.)

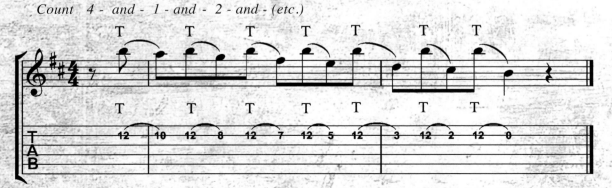

In the example at the bottom of page 62, the tapping finger stays on the same fret (12th) while the left hand moves down the neck! The phrase starts on the quaver upbeat (count 4-*and*) before the first full bar. Use your fourth finger on the 10th fret, then second finger, and then first finger for the other left-hand notes, moving swiftly between every right-hand tap.

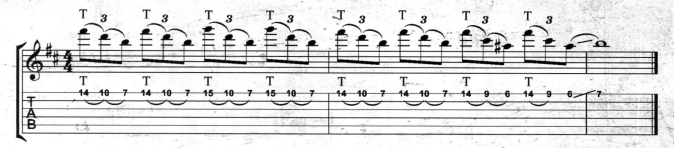

For the third example, let's try out a different three-note combination. Tapping on the 14th fret of the top string, you subsequently pull off to your fourth finger on the 10th fret. This move is quickly followed by another pull-off, from the 10th fret to your first finger on the 7th. For the next shape, simply move your tapping finger to the 15th fret, and perform the same left-hand pull-offs as before. You then come back to tapping the 14th fret—and finish by moving the left-hand shape one fret back (while still tapping the 14th fret) and performing a 6th-to-7th-fret slide using the first finger. Happy practicing.

TRACKS FEATURING TAPPING

Eddie Van Halen (Van Halen): "Eruption"—
    Van Halen (1978)
Andy McKee: "Drifting"—*Art of Motion* (2005)
Buckethead: "The Ballad of Buckethead"—
    Monsters and Robots (1999)
Guthrie Govan: "Fives"—live version on
    Lee Ritenour's *6 String Theory* (2010)

Right: Buckethead—a.k.a. Brian Carroll—often uses virtuoso tapping in his solos.

Eddie Van Halen

TAPPING

NOW IT'S TIME to try our hand at a challenging example in the style of tapping pioneer Eddie Van Halen. Many people see Eddie as tapping's original master, and he certainly blew a lot of minds with the instrumental track "Eruption" (1978)—a stunning display of virtuosic tapping unlikely anything most people had ever heard before!

Our example features the already familiar "tap + pull-off + hammer-on" combination exclusively, so that's good news. The greatest challenge comes from the fact that both your left hand *and* your tapping finger move positions throughout! So put on your "intense concentration face" and let's dig in. Starting on the 12th fret of the 2nd string, the first pattern stretches over two bars, using the tapping finger and the first and fourth fingers on your left hand. Basically, you keep tapping on the 12th fret, while your left hand changes position, descending one fret at a time, and maintaining the first and fourth finger combination. (In fact, you can use this fingering throughout the piece.) In bars 3 and 4, the same principle applies, only this time the whole thing is played two frets lower —thus tapping on the 10th fret, and (in bar 3) pulling off to the 5th and hammering on to the 8th. So far, so good! Next comes a series of arpeggios, providing some interesting harmony: note that even though both left hand and tapping finger positions change constantly, they *never change at the same time*! So whenever your left hand moves to a new position, your tapping finger stays tapping the same fret—and whenever your tapping finger moves to a new fret, your left hand stays in the same position during that change. For the last bar, see if you can produce a nice long final note with your tapping finger. Well done!

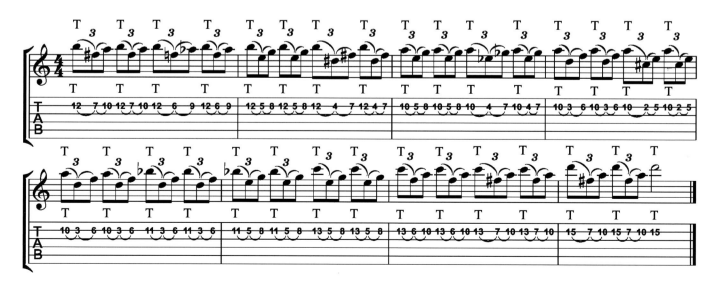

Eddie Van Halen was born in Amsterdam in 1955, but moved to the United States with his family as a child. The Van Halens settled in Pasadena, California, where Eddie and his brother **Alex** (b.1953) became known for their musical skills; their father, **Jan** (1920–86), was a bandleader and sax/clarinet player. In 1972, the siblings formed a group initially called **Mammoth** but soon renamed **Van Halen**, with Eddie on guitar and Alex as drummer (at one time, their choice of instruments had been reversed). Their self-titled 1978 debut album won Eddie international recognition for his agile, powerful playing—whose technical secrets he sometimes tried to conceal from live audiences by turning his back on them!

Van Halen—dominated by Eddie and vocalist **David Lee Roth**—produced five more best-selling albums over the next six years; during this period, Eddie also contributed his celebrated guitar solo to **Michael Jackson's** "Beat It" (*Thriller*, 1982). Roth left Van Halen following the release of *1984* (named for its issue date); his replacement, **Sammy Hagar**, was to remain with the band until 1996. That year saw a short-lived, stormy reunion with Roth; in its aftermath, **Gary Cherone** was brought in to provide vocals, while Hagar rejoined the group for their 2004 concert dates across the U.S. and Canada. David Lee Roth eventually returned for Van Halen's triumphant 2007–08 North American tour on which Eddie's son, **Wolfgang**, served as bassist in place of **Michael Anthony**.

Over the years, Eddie has faced serious health worries: he underwent hip replacement surgery in 1999, was successfully treated for oral cancer at the start of the new century, and has also been in rehab. More recently, though, he's been keeping a higher profile, thanks in part to the promotion of his **EVH** range of equipment and merchandise, manufactured by Fender, and including guitars, amps, pickups, and accessories such as plectrums and cables. In the past, Eddie's been associated with several other brands—from axes by Charvel, Kramer, and Ernie Ball/Music Man to amplification by Marshall and Peavey.

Hybrid Picking

HYBRID PICKING combines the regular method of picking we've been using so far with elements of fingerpicking. It's very popular in country and bluegrass, but is also part of the "technical vocabulary" of modern day Rock Guitar wizards like Eric Johnson (*see* page 68) and Buckethead (*see* page 63). Providing you hold your plectrum between your index finger and thumb, it enables you to strike strings with your other three right-hand fingers as well—and makes a technique such as string skipping, which we've already heard about, *much* easier to execute.

The example below demonstrates how you can use hybrid picking on chords and arpeggios. Section A features a B5 power chord, followed by the same chord with an A in its bass. We play all the notes on the 5th string with the pick, and fingerpick the notes at the 4th fret of the 4th and 3rd strings with, respectively, our middle (m) and ring (a) fingers. This is definitely a challenging combination for both brain and hand —don't expect it to feel natural straight away! As regards fretting, I'd opt for first finger on the 5th string, and third and fourth on the 4th and 3rd strings.

PIMAC

The most widely used method of showing right-hand guitar fingerings is **PIMAC**—an acronym for the names of the five digits.

P = pulgar (thumb)
I = index
M = middle (or medio)
A = annular (ring)
C = "chiquita" (little)

These letters, printed above the stave, indicate the fingers you should use to pick specific notes. "Chiquita" only appears very occasionally.

Right: James Burton has a well-deserved reputation as one of the world's finest guitar pickers in either rock or country music.

For section B (*see* opposite), all fingerings stay the same, but here we play one string at a time, while still adhering to the principle of picking the A string and fingerpicking the D and G strings.

In section C, we switch to a B minor chord—and bring in the little finger ("c" for chiquita) as well. The first chord is played by simultaneously picking the A, D, G and B strings, using the plectrum as well as all the other available right-hand fingers. For the arpeggiated chord lines, the combination of pick, middle, and ring finger is deployed to great effect. Left-hand fingerings stay the same, with the added second finger playing on the B string.

This next example (below) demonstrates how useful hybrid picking can be for soloing lines. Bars 1 and 2 feature a cool sequential lick. Start by plucking the 3rd string with your middle finger (m); then pick the 4th string and pull-off/hammer-on straight away. As you move onward, the pattern's starting note changes every time. In bars 3 and 4, we begin with two notes played simultaneously, using a first-finger bar in bar 3. To finish, we play three intervals (sixths), using pick and middle finger. Left-hand fingerings: first (G string) and second finger for the first two sixths, and third (G string) and second finger for the last interval.

Remember, this technique isn't for everyone! Some guitarists put it to great use, but others never employ it at all.

HYBRID PICKING TRACKS

Eric Johnson: "Manhattan"—*G3 Live in Concert* (1997), originally on *Venus Isle* (1996)
James Burton: "Mystery Train"—*The Guitar Sounds of James Burton* (1971)
Buckethead: "Jordan"—downloadable single (2009), originally featured on *Guitar Hero II*
Stevie Ray Vaughan: "Lenny"—*Texas Flood* (1983)

Right: Stevie Ray Vaughan—his death in a flying accident in 1990 was a sad loss to rock and blues.

Eric Johnson

HYBRID PICKING

"Sometimes you just keep pushing…to develop your own signature sound and style."

NOW LET'S ZOOM in on all-round guitar virtuoso Eric Johnson, who uses hybrid picking as a natural, highly integrated component of his style. Remember I made reference to country? Well, have a listen to "Steve's Boogie" from Eric's popular *Ah Via Musicom* album (1990) for a taste of this. Make sure you also check out "Cliffs of Dover"—now a playable track on *Guitar Hero III*!

Our Johnson-inspired example starts with a mighty string-skipped lick, spanning two bars. Placing your fourth finger on the 14th fret of the B string to start, you fingerpick the 10th fret on the high E string as every second note from then on—using your first finger to fret it and your middle finger (m) to strike it. (You could also pick with your ring finger [a] if you find that more comfortable.) Other left-hand fingerings: use your fourth finger on any 14th fret notes, and second or third finger for 12th fret.

Bar 3 kicks off with an Em9 chord, and here we need to enlist the services of our right hand "pinky." Play the chord on the first beat (an Em7) using pick, middle (m), and ring finger (a)—then strike an F# (creating an Em9) from the 14th fret of the E string with your little finger, while allowing the previous notes to ring on. To fret these notes, use fingers 2, 1, 4, and 3 (from the 4th string up). Then we get 12th on the 5th string and 12th on the high E string, with a huge gap in between: use pick and ring finger (a) to play this, saving your middle finger

(m) for the 12th on the 2nd string after it. You can play this effectively by barring the 12th fret with your first finger.

The last bar is a nice Hendrix-y phrase using your plectrum on the 5th string (first finger to fret) and your ring finger to pick the note on the 15th fret of the 2nd string. We continue with a hammer-on and a pull-off, fretted with your second and fourth fingers. Finish by striking the G string (16th fret) with your middle finger (m), using the pick for the final note. This is pretty advanced stuff, so be sure to take your time with it.

Happy practicing!

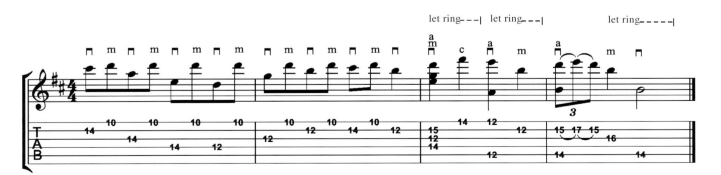

Eric Johnson is from Austin, Texas. He was born in 1954, and started playing the piano as a five-year-old, switching to guitar about seven years later. His influences took in rock, country (through the work of **Chet Atkins**), jazz (via **Django Reinhardt**, and **John McLaughlin** of the **Mahavishnu Orchestra**), and blues. In his mid-teens, he became a member of psychedelic "power trio" **Mariani**, named for its drummer, **Vince Mariani**. They put out a single, "Re-Birth Day," on a local Austin label, Sonobeat, in 1970, and, with a different line-up, made an album for that company the same year. Entitled *Perpetuum Mobile*, and now available on CD, it features some striking Echoplex tape-delay effects on Johnson's guitar.

Johnson joined the **Electromagnets**—characterized by **Frank Zappa** as "a Mahavishnu [Orchestra] with a sense of humor"—in 1974. The band, which never achieved the success it deserved, recorded two LPs; after its demise, Eric launched a trio of his own with former Electromagnets **Kyle Brock** (bass) and **Bill Maddox** (drums). Their album *Seven Worlds* dates from 1976–77, but remained unreleased until 1998, and Johnson had to wait until the mid-1980s for a contract with a major label (Warner Bros.) His sole CD for Warners, *Tones* (1986), received critical acclaim, but it took four more years and another change of label before he hit the big time with his platinum-selling *Ah Via Musicom* (1990). Eric is a painstaking perfectionist, and there have been lengthy intervals between his solo albums, though he is constantly busy with a range of musical enterprises—from his "side-project" blues band, **Alien Love Child** (for which his regular collaborator **Bill Maddox**, who died in December 2010, was the drummer), to **G3** tour dates with **Joe Satriani** and **Steve Vai**. His sixth solo studio album, *Up Close*, appeared in 2010.

A long-time Fender Stratocaster player, Eric Johnson uses an amp set-up incorporating Fender Twin Reverbs and Marshalls.

Natural Harmonics

Right: Harmonics are produced with a gentle touch above the fret.

OUR NEXT TOPIC is **harmonics**, and without getting all scientific about it, I'll start by saying they are *great* fun to play with! Whether you use harmonics to create bell-like notes, loud squeals, or crazy effects, they'll always stand out due to their unique sound quality. The easiest ones to produce are the **natural harmonics**, which you can find in several places across the fretboard.

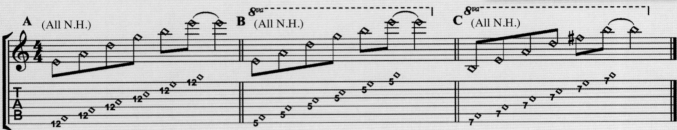

In example A (above), we see the line of harmonics you can play across all six strings on your 12th fret. The important thing with harmonics is that we generally find them *on* the fret, rather than *between* the frets—so you must steer your left hand (use its first finger here) to the *right* of the 12th fret (directly over the fret wire), and just *lightly* touch the string, without actually pushing down on it. The string doesn't need to make contact with the fret. In contrast to your left hand's light touch, you need a fairly strong picking motion in your right hand. I suggest letting your pick "fall" onto the next string, really squeezing down on each string as it's played. After making contact with the string at the correct place on the fretboard, you can take your finger off again—and the note should still be ringing. Using the bridge pickup will help bring out the harmonic.

Now try the same thing at the *5th* fret in example B. As you may notice, the notes are all the same, except they're sounding one octave higher. This is due to the various "nodal" points along the string, which we'll explore further later, as we dive deeper into harmonics.

Finally, example C has us making the same moves, but this time at the *7th* fret, which produces an entirely different group of notes. Before you move on, play around with all these, mixing up all three examples—and maybe even making up some little riffs. The low E string combined with any of these harmonics should give you hours of fun.

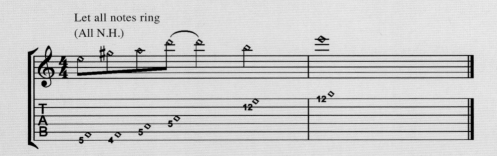

Our second example (left) is a cool little phrase, which uses some of the natural harmonics we've already discovered—as well as a harmonic at the 4th fret of the bottom E string. Fingering-wise, I'd use 2, 1, and then 2 for the rest of the notes— letting all the notes ring out (except the very first one, which is stopped by the following note on the same string). It's a pretty awesome sound, right?

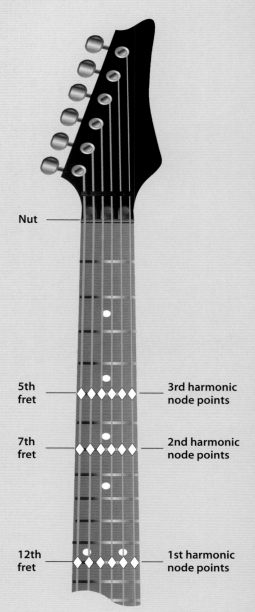

Nut

5th fret — 3rd harmonic node points

7th fret — 2nd harmonic node points

12th fret — 1st harmonic node points

Above: These are the main locations for the guitar's natural harmonics. They're indicated in notation using a hollow diamond symbol (◇) and the abbreviation N.H.

TRACKS FEATURING HARMONICS

Billy Gibbons (ZZ Top): "La Grange"—*Tres Hombres* (1973)

Brad Delson (Linkin Park): "One Step Closer"— *Hybrid Theory* (2000)

Randy Rhoads (Ozzy Osbourne): "Crazy Train"— *Blizzard of Ozz* (1980); there's a great live version on *Tribute* (1987) as well

Zakk Wylde (Black Label Society): "Black Sunday"— *Order of the Black* (2010)

Richie Sambora (Bon Jovi): "Wanted Dead or Alive"— *Slippery When Wet* (1986)

Above: Zakk Wylde's "bullseye"-finish guitars are made by Gibson. However, cheaper versions are produced by its Epiphone subsidiary.

Billy Gibbons

HARMONICS

"Turn on, tune up, rock out."

NEXT WE TAKE a look at **artificial harmonics**, a.k.a. **pinch harmonics** or *"squealies"*…and how better to illustrate them than via the awesome rock style of long-time (and long-bearded!) ZZ Top guitarist Billy Gibbons?

To produce an artificial/pinch harmonic, abbreviated in the notation as A.H., and indicated in tablature with a solid diamond notehead ♦ (regular notation uses the same noteheads for natural and artificial harmonics), we need to touch the string lightly with our right-hand thumb, immediately after the pick has made contact with the string, and then take it off again very quickly. Furthermore, we must pick the string at a particular place in relation to the location of the note we're fretting with our left hand. Basically, certain spots ("node points") along the string will generate certain notes, so in principle you can keep your left hand stationary and produce several different notes just by picking different points on the string using the pinch-harmonic technique. The most common pinch harmonics are the ones you can find **one** or **two octaves** higher then the fretted note—the equivalent of *12* or *24* frets above it.

Before we start, do yourself a favor and add a truckload of distortion to your sound; this will make it tons easier!

Our example is based on the G minor pentatonic scale, and we'll be using the harmonics you find two octaves above the fretted notes. The whole phrase stays within the familiar

*Right: Striking the
first pinch harmonic
in the notation below.
The position where it's
picked varies slightly
from guitar to guitar.*

position of the scale, and our main challenge is finding the right place to pick the string, in relation to the notes we are fretting. For the first pinch harmonic in the first bar, we've got our third finger on the 5th fret of the 4th string. Now go and "search" for the right place to pick—executing the pinch-harmonic technique somewhere in the area above your neck pickup, because this is where this harmonic can be found on most guitars. Bends start to appear in the 3rd bar (refer to the bending section on pages 50–53 if necessary); here we combine the pinch harmonic and a bend, and occasionally bend without a harmonic. Don't forget that you'll have to move your string-picking position to the right in order to produce the harmonics two octaves above the different notes you're fretting. Then finish off with a nice long pinch harmonic on the 3rd fret—remembering to move your right-hand picking spot slightly to the left, and adding that cool vibrato to make the note really sing. Nice!

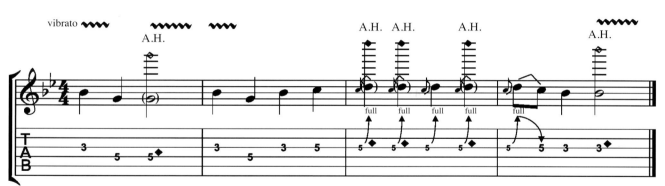

Billy F. Gibbons was born in Tanglewood, part of the Uptown western suburb of Houston, Texas, on December 16, 1949. He shares his middle name, Frederick, with his father (1908–81), a pianist and bandleader who formerly provided live backing for silent movies. Billy's musical skills manifested themselves from an early age, and he acquired his first electric guitar, a Gibson Melody Maker (also the choice, a few years later, of **Runaways**' leader **Joan Jett**) when he was just 13.

Inspired by **Elvis Presley**, **Jimmy Reed**, and (especially) bluesman **McKinley Morganfield**, a.k.a. **Muddy Waters**, Billy Gibbons quickly became an integral part of his local music scene. In 1967, his group **The Moving Sidewalks** had a regional hit with one of his songs, "99th Floor;" a year later they were hired to support **The Jimi Hendrix Experience** for several U.S. tour dates, and Jimi endorsed Billy as an emerging talent. The young guitarist's musical future, though, lay not with the psychedelia of the Sidewalks, who split up in 1969, but in the bluesier, Tex-Mex-flavored style epitomized by **ZZ Top**. The all-Texan trio, also featuring

Dusty Hill (bass) and **Frank Beard** (drums), made their concert debut in February 1970, and recorded their first LP the same year. The band's fame grew steadily throughout the decade (their first hit single, "La Grange," came from their 1973 album, *Tres Hombres*), but reached its zenith in the 1980s, when their combination of musical potency and distinctive visual style made them favorites on MTV, which had launched in 1981. Their most successful album, currently certified as 10x platinum (having sold over 3,000,000 worldwide) is *Eliminator*, released in 1983, and including classic numbers, such as "Legs" and "Sharp Dressed Man;" but subsequent records and sell-out tours have kept them at the forefront of rock—an impressive achievement for an outfit that has remained together, with no personnel changes, for over 40 years.

Billy Gibbons has a vast collection of guitars—in a recent interview he described them as "my raison d'être"— but the one he loves most is his 1959 Les Paul Standard, nicknamed "Pearly Gates," and recently produced in a replica custom edition by Gibson. He uses Marshall amplification.

Advanced Harmonics

NOW WE'RE getting into some pretty advanced territory, and exploring techniques that will take some time to master…but will provide you with tools for creating truly special sounds and phrases. Beware, though—the price to pay for mastering techniques like these is likely to be many, many hours of practicing. That said, let's have some fun!

First we'll look at harmonics that can be tapped (**tap harmonics**), or just touched (**touch harmonics**). They're abbreviated—not surprisingly—as T.H., and notated with a solid diamond. I recommend adding *loads* of distortion to all the following examples!

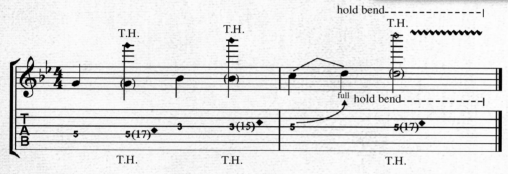

Above: This technique produces a touch harmonic from the node point at the 17th fret on the 4th string.

Below: George Lynch, former lead guitarist with heavy metal band Dokken, at a Hollywood gig in 2009.

Tap harmonics were made popular by Eddie Van Halen, and are really a natural extension of the tapping technique. This example (above) uses the G minor pentatonic scale, and is similar to the Billy Gibbons-style item on pages 72–73. Here, however, the harmonic "node point" that we'll use is just **one** octave (12 frets) above the fretted notes. So, in the first bar, when you're fretting at the 5th fret with your left hand (third finger), you need to find the node point on the 17th fret (5+12 =17). First, give this example a go using **touch harmonics**— where you just touch the string lightly above the 17th fret after

striking the 5th fret. You can use any finger for this, but I'd go for the middle finger. Then try it out using **tap harmonics**, where you tap on the same node point instead, coming off it again fairly quickly. The last bar is a classic EVH move, where we first bend up to a note, and then *whack* it up an octave by tapping (or touching) the harmonic node point. We finish by holding the bend and giving it a victorious vibrato!

Now let's dive further into the intricacies of the tap harmonics technique, and explore *more* node points along the length of the string.

This example shows how we can produce different notes by holding down a note—5th fret on the 4th string—and tapping at various harmonic node points along the string—17th, 12th, and 9th frets. This essentially produces a G major arpeggio, even though our left hand is only fretting a single G! In contrast to the previous example, where each note is fretted and *then* "made into a harmonic," we're tapping the harmonic straight away—thus, you may need to practice the tapping motion for a while, because great precision and a little more force is needed to produce the notes.

Finally, let's really go exploring those harmonic node points along the string.

Here, we get a trill going in our left hand (use the first and third fingers) on the low E string. While you're trilling, gently touch the string with any finger on your right hand, just like when you produced touch harmonics on the fretboard. This time, though, start at the bridge end of the string and then slowly move your finger along the string, hearing how various harmonic nodal points occur. Keep going all the way down the string and back up again. A great example of this can be heard just before the main theme at the start of Joe Satriani's "Motorcycle Driver." Sounds cool, right?

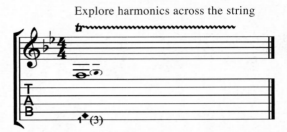

Right: Eddie Van Halen, stripped to the waist for action, and flourishing one of his custom guitars.

TRACKS FEATURING ADVANCED HARMONICS

Andy Summers (Police): "Can't Stand Losing You"—
    Outlandos d'Amour (1978)
Eddie Van Halen (Michael Jackson): "Beat It"—*Thriller* (1982)
Joe Satriani: "Motorcycle Driver"—*The Extremist* (1992)
George Lynch (Dokken): "In My Dreams"—
    Under Lock and Key (1985)

Andy Summers

HARP HARMONICS

"My favorite sounds are the high, spacey ones that are very ambient."

HARP HARMONICS hark back to guitar greats like Lenny Breau and Chet Atkins, while Andy Summers from The Police is one of the most prominent rock players using them: check out the "bridge" (middle section) of "Can't Stand Losing You." The technique, also known as **chime harmonics**, takes time to master, but is an extremely beautiful tool to have in your arsenal, should you possess the patience to learn how to do it well.

Abbreviated in the notation as H.H., they involve fretting a note with your left hand, holding a right-hand finger (usually the index finger) over the harmonic node point (most commonly 12 frets above the note you are fretting), and then picking this note, either with one of your other right-hand fingers or your pick.

If the picking is executed by your thumb, it would look like this:

Left: A harp or chime harmonic struck with the right-hand thumb.

And if you decided to use your pick, you'd be holding it between your thumb and middle finger, leaving the index finger free to touch the desired harmonic node point, like this:

Left: Gripping the pick like this frees up your right-hand index finger to touch the string.

Our notated example is fairly simple for your left hand, which just holds down a bar on the 3rd fret, covering all strings with its first finger. Remember to use the thumb to find a comfortable position, pressing it against the back of the fretboard. I would use a clean sound, letting the notes ring freely. Don't be afraid to turn up the volume quite a bit, because this will make producing the harmonics easier for you. The neighbors shouldn't care; after all, it will eventually sound all beautiful and harp-like!

So, what we'll do here is hold down the chord and then alternately strike the harmonics and the regular notes—lightly touching the string 12 frets above the fretted notes when picking the harmonics.

Let all notes ring

Let's use the first finger on each harmonic nodal point, the thumb to pick the harmonic, and our ring finger to pick the regular notes. Alternatively, use the plectrum for the harmonics instead of the thumb. Practice this v-e-r-y slowly, boiling it down to "sets"—one harmonic and one regular note at a time. This way, you'll get used to alternating between harmonics and regular notes much faster.

The next step would be trying this out on *other* chords— soon you could be making sounds reminiscent of church bells ringing! I don't suppose you imagined *that* sound coming out of your guitar when you first picked it up?

Andy Summers was born on New Year's Eve, 1942, and grew up in the English seaside resort of Bournemouth. A self-taught guitarist, he made friends, during his teenage years, with other local musicians (notably **Robert Fripp**, soon to be famous as co-founder of **King Crimson**), but had established himself in London by the mid-1960s. He enjoyed early successes with bands led by British rhythm-and-blues stalwarts **Zoot Money** and **Eric Burdon**, was a prolific session player, and spent several years in the United States, where he studied classical guitar at college in California.

Back in the U.K., Summers joined a four-piece line-up of **The Police** in the summer of 1977; he'd previously worked with bassist **Sting** (Gordon Sumner) in a band called **Strontium 90**. Within a few months, The Police became a trio, following the departure of guitarist **Henry Padovani**, and they released their debut album, *Outlandos D'Amour*, in November 1978. Made on a budget of just $6,000, it contained the band's first hit singles—"Roxanne," "Can't

Stand Losing You," and "So Lonely"—and eventually went platinum. The Police achieved massive worldwide popularity and huge record sales; *Synchronicity* (1983), their fifth and last studio LP, was also their biggest seller, reaching No.1 in the U.K. and U.S. album charts, and featuring what was probably their most celebrated song, "Every Breath You Take."

While still with The Police, Summers made a memorable album in collaboration with his old friend and fellow guitar wizard Robert Fripp (*I Advance Masked*, 1982); and since the band split up in 1984, he has retained a high musical profile as a soloist and sideman. Especially notable from a guitarist's perspective are his album of duets with jazzman **John Etheridge** (*Invisible Threads*, 1993), and his guest appearance on Cuban classical player **Manuel Barrueco's** *Nylon and Steel* (2001). The instrument most closely associated with him is his 1961 Fender Telecaster (issued as a limited edition replica by Fender in 2007); his favorite amps include Roland Jazz Chorus combos and Mesa Boogies.

The Whammy Bar

OUR NEXT TOPIC is the amazing tool (and toy!) that is the **whammy bar**. Starting out as a handy way of producing vibrato, it evolved rapidly in the hands of guitarists like Jimi Hendrix and Jeff Beck, enabling players to imitate everything from dive bombers to horses, revving engines, and even talking (listen to Steve Vai's "The Audience Is Listening" from *Passion & Warfare* [1990] for that one!) There are several different types of whammy-bar system. However, many rock guitarists favor the **floating**, **double-locking** system. "Floating" means the bar can go both down (to lower the pitch) and up (to raise the pitch). "Double-locking" means that the strings are locked at both the bridge *and* nut, which greatly increases tuning stability. The following examples will work best if you have a floating system, but most can be played even if you don't—and without double-locking, you'll need to re-tune very frequently. We'll use the G minor pentatonic scale throughout…and let's add lots of distortion for increased sustain. Also, pay close attention to muting the strings you aren't playing, using your left hand.

Let's start by performing **dips** (right). After striking the note (using your third finger on the D string's 5th fret), simply lower the whammy bar a little, and then release it again, performing repeated dips. At first, try lowering it by just a semitone or half-step, as shown in the notation by the "V" and "– 1/2" symbols. Then try much deeper dips (two steps or tones, a fifth, etc.). Next, experiment with different ways of working the bar; you can hold on to it and push it down, or you can hit it with your palm or the side of your hand. Lastly, if you have a floating system, try turning the bar so it points away from the neck. This raises the pitch instead of lowering it, producing a slightly Eastern feel. Be gentle, though—these inverted dips will break your strings if you push down too far.

Left: The author's Hamer guitar, fitted with a floating Floyd Rose whammy-bar set-up.

For the example above, you need to grab the whammy bar and hold it between your index and middle fingers while picking the notes. On each of the first three notes we perform a **scoop** (notated as a ✓), which involves pressing down on the bar, and releasing it just as you've picked each note. The final note is a **gargle**, which you need a decent floating system to execute. As the note is ringing, flick the tip of the whammy bar with your hand so that the system trembles for a split second. Steve Vai is a master of the technique. Use left-hand fingers 3, 1, and 3 for this example.

Finally, we'll try the classic **dive-bombing** effect (below)! For example A, we simply hit the low E string and depress the whammy bar until it can't go any further. Example B is a screaming dive-bomb sound, achieved by hitting the natural harmonic over the 5th fret of the G string and—again—pushing the bar all the way down. Example C provides a slight variation on this, and is played with a pinch harmonic (which on most guitars can be found between the end of the fretboard and the neck pickup). When you're comfortable with the initial dive-bomb, try creating the **horse** effect associated with guitarists like Eddie Van Halen and Steve Vai. To emulate a whinnying horse, produce the harmonic, then shake the bar while gradually pressing it further and further down. It's a whole new dimension!

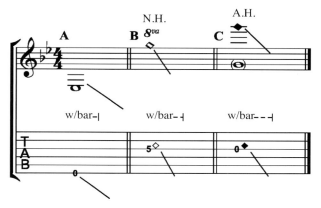

THE WHAMMY BAR IN ACTION

Jeff Beck: "Led Boots"—*Performing This Week…Live at Ronnie Scott's Jazz Club* (2008)
Jimi Hendrix: "Star Spangled Banner"—*Live at Woodstock* (1999)
Steve Vai: "Bad Horsie"—*Alien Love Secrets* (1995)
Joe Satriani: "Satch Boogie"—*Surfing with the Alien* (1987)

Left: Steve Vai's Ibanez is another model that sports a floating vibrato ("trem") system.

Jeff Beck

THE WHAMMY BAR

"I play the way I do because it allows me to come up with the sickest sounds possible."

JEFF BECK IS an absolute master of the whammy bar, and his creative use of it forms a considerable part of his extremely original playing style. Let's zoom in on some of the techniques Jeff likes to feature. Bear in mind that he usually plays with his fingers rather than a pick, which has an effect on his sound. Also, Jeff uses a floating bridge, and if you don't have one of those bad boys, you shouldn't expect to be able to perform these maneuvers to perfection. That said, you can still get a taste of his amazing whammy-bar phrasings.

Our example is based on the G minor pentatonic scale, in the position we're quite familiar with—only this time it's an octave higher. Fingering-wise, that means our left-hand first finger generally plays the notes at the 15th fret, third finger tackles notes at the 17th, and fourth handles those at the 18th.

We start off with two scoops, so remember to grab the whammy bar between your index and middle fingers before even playing the first note. After the scoops, we get a nice lick, which starts with four notes (including a hammer-on), and ends with the fourth note ringing and then getting forcefully shaken, whammy-bar style! Depending on your type of whammy-bar system, this will probably require a solid grip of the bar, and the use of your whole arm to shake it.

I find that grabbing the bar with my palm, and holding it between my ring and little fingers only, gives me more space for really deep dives and returns, without fear of knocking my knuckle on the guitar. In bar 2, the lick is repeated, and followed by another two scoops. This time, insert a break between them—and note that the second scoop is followed immediately by a hammer-on. As always, focus in on little bits like this, and practice them separately.

Next we get a bend and added vibrato, preceded by a scoop. So, first depress the whammy bar—then pick the note. As you're releasing the whammy bar, start doing the bend, so that the bar will have returned to its original position by the time the bend is full. Remember to support it with the remaining left-hand fingers, as explained in the bending section on pages 50–53.

Then we get another four-note legato lick that leaves the last note ringing and open for whammy-bar manipulation. This time, we're going to tap or hit the actual *bridge* instead of using the whammy bar, making the note vibrate quickly up and down. This is one of Jeff Beck's signature moves, and you really need a floating bridge to make it happen, as the pitch is raised, not lowered. I recommend using the area of your hand where

the palm meets the wrist to tap on the bridge, but by all means experiment with other techniques. You could try hitting it with the downside of your closed fist, or with just one finger…it all depends on how your bridge is set up, and how you choose to hit it. To finish, we simply play the legato phrase, and then (in bar 4) move the first finger down to the 13th fret, depressing the whammy bar to make a final dive. Pretty awesome, right!

Jeff Beck was born at Wallington in Surrey in 1944. His formative influences included rock and roll, blues, and jazz, and after a short spell at art college, he embarked on a musical career in the early 1960s. It was his friend and fellow session-player **Jimmy Page** who advised **The Yardbirds** to recruit him as a replacement for **Eric Clapton** in March 1965. For a brief period in 1966, Beck and Page were both members of The Yardbirds (*see* pages 28–9), and Page also composed "Beck's Bolero"—which its dedicatee recorded in 1966 with Page, bassist **John Paul Jones** (soon, like Page, to be part of Led Zeppelin) and **The Who's Keith Moon**. It appeared on the B-side of Beck's first post-Yardbirds single, "Hi Ho Silver Lining" (1967). **The Jeff Beck Group**, established the same year, featured future **Faces Rod Stewart** and **Ronnie Wood**; they disbanded in summer 1969 after recording two albums, *Truth* (1968) and *Beck-Ola* (1969), and Beck's career was temporarily stalled when he was injured in a car crash that December.

Having regained his health, Beck went on to form a new **Jeff Beck Group**, and then a "power trio" with bassist **Tim Bogert** and drummer **Carmine Appice**; however, the guitarist's major artistic and commercial breakthroughs came with his platinum-selling jazz-fusion style albums, *Blow by Blow* (1975) and *Wired* (1976). His work in the last two decades of the twentieth century was punctuated by less musically active spells, but the techno-influenced CDs, *Who Else!* (1999) and *You Had It Coming* (2001), were exciting departures, and his continuing energy and creativity have been evident on recent tours and recordings. They've also been recognized at the Grammys, where Beck's numerous awards have included those for "Best Rock Instrumental Performance" and "Best Pop Instrumental Performance" in 2011—both given to tracks from his album *Emotion & Commotion* (2010).

Jeff Beck is a long-time Fender Stratocaster player, who uses Fender and Marshall amps.

Drop D Tuning

ROP D TUNING is the most popular alternative way to tune amongst rock guitarists. It's quite simple: all you do is drop your low E string down a whole step or tone (to D—hence the name). This gives us a nice low D, and a whole new set of possibilities to play with. From "Moby Dick" (Led Zeppelin's Jimmy Page) to "Optimistic" (Radiohead's Jonny Greenwood) and onward, Drop D tuning is all over *Rock Guitar*! It features frequently in hard rock and heavy metal—as power chords become very easy to play in Drop D, making way for killer riffs with superfast transitions. It's also used by acoustic guitar wizards like John Martyn, Eric Roche, and Newton Faulkner. It's worth mentioning that if you play in Drop D a lot, you should consider using a heavier gauge of string for the low E string, because it'll be less likely to get pushed out of tune when fretted, and will generally sound better.

In example A (left), we basically tune the low E string to D. There are various ways you can do this—using a tuner is the easiest method, of course. Another way is "matching" the low E string with the D (4th) string: although they'll be one octave apart, they will sound "locked in" when they're both tuned to a D (albeit in different octaves). When you've tuned the string, try example B, which is a standard open D chord, but now sports a mighty-sounding low D as its lowest note.

OK, in this example (below) we'll explore the joy of having that low D to play with. It's picked on every downbeat, alternating with descending notes from the D major scale on the upbeats. I suggest using your third finger on the 12th fret, and then your first finger for all other notes—until the slide (7th to 9th fret), which I'd play with my third finger. After the slide, give the note some nice vibrato against the low backdrop of the ringing D. Awesome!

Top right: Dave Grohl sometimes performs the Drop D classic "Everlong" on an acoustic guitar.

Above: The slide from E to the final F# in the example shown opposite above.

Let all notes ring

82

Now, let's switch on some distortion and find out just how well Drop D tuning works with power-chord riffing…

Playing on your lowest two strings throughout (above), you can use your first finger to bar and fret all of the chords. Alternatively, involve your other fingers—like third finger on the 5th fret and fourth finger on the 6th…or any other combination you prefer. Notice the **palm muting** in bar 2. Here, we want to let our palm touch and partially mute the strings down by the bridge as we pick them. This is extremely common in rock and metal, so make sure you practice switching between regular picking and palm-muted picking. Have fun rocking out with this one!

Below: Mike Einziger of Incubus, another exponent of Drop D, onstage with his modified Gibson SG.

Bottom left: Matt Bellamy from Muse in full flight!

TRACKS FEATURING DROP D

Tom Morello (Rage Against The Machine): "Killing In The Name"—*Rage Against The Machine* (1992)

Daron Malakian (System Of A Down): "Aerials"—*Toxicity* (2001)

Matt Bellamy (Muse): "Feeling Good"—*Origin Of Symmetry* (2001)

Adam Jones (Tool): "Schism"—*Lateralus* (2001)

Kurt Cobain (Nirvana): "Heart-Shaped Box"—*In Utero* (1993)

Dave Grohl (Foo Fighters): "Everlong"—*The Colour and the Shape* (1997)

Kim Thayil (Soundgarden): "Spoonman"—*Superunknown* (1994)

Mike Einziger (Incubus): "Redefine"—*S.C.I.E.N.C.E.* (1997)

Tom Morello

DROP D

"We offer a stark contrast to the bland escapism that chokes the charts."

NOW LET'S ZOOM in on Rock Guitar wizard **Tom Morello**, who—aside from being a brilliantly creative guitarist—is also a serial Drop D user. Whether with **Rage Against The Machine**, **Audioslave**, or others, he's always been able to deliver some seriously awesome and hard-hitting rock riffs based on Drop D tuning. So, let's have a look at our Morello-style example, which—as Tom's riffs often do—combines a number of elements: big fat power chords, single lines, "dead" notes, and power-chord slides.

We start off with two massive-sounding power chords, open D5 and then F5, which I'd fret by barring with my first finger. Then we play a single-note line—where I'd use first finger on 3rd fret, and hammer-on to 5th fret with my third finger. This is quickly followed by two strums—a downstroke and an upstroke—on "dead" notes (marked as "x" in notation and tab). You get these by lightly resting your left hand across the strings without actually fretting any notes. I suggest using all your fingers for this, to ensure that (even though we're only hitting the two lowest strings) we don't hear unwanted notes if we accidentally strum any others. Your left hand can mute the strings anywhere along the neck, but I suggest you stay where you already are (around the 5th fret). Also, look out for natural harmonics: you don't want these ringing out accidentally. Next comes a power-chord slide, from 2nd to 3rd fret of the 5th and 6th strings. I'd perform this with my first finger, quickly moving back to the 2nd fret and picking the bar's final power chord.

Bar 2 starts the same way as the first bar, and then has a nice big break. Bar 3 is the same as bar 1, and builds up nicely to the fourth bar, which—like all previous bars—starts with a big fat D5 power chord. For the last part of this four-bar riff, we play 12th fret on the 6th string, continuing with a pull-off to that nice low D, and following up promptly with a C5 power chord on the 10th fret. Again, the power chord is easily played by barring with your first finger. To finish off, we strum twice on another set of dead notes (same technique, different place on the neck), before hitting another C5 power chord.

Make sure you practice this riff really slowly and (if necessary) in little bits at a time, focusing on getting the *timing* as well as the *combination of techniques* right. Then repeat *ad libitum* until your neighbors complain! Happy rockin'—and enjoy the headbanging!

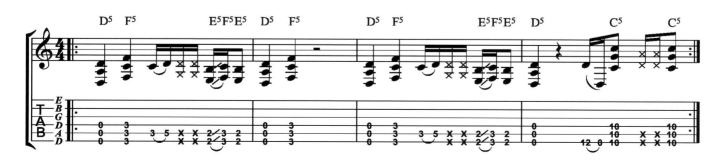

Tom Morello (b.1964) is a New Yorker by birth, but he grew up in Chicago. The paternal side of his family are Kenyans with a history of involvement in politics, and Morello himself, a Harvard graduate, creates music that engages with social and political issues in a way that sometimes harks back to singer-songwriter **Woody Guthrie** (1912–67)— composer of "This Land is Your Land" (performed by Morello when he appears as **The Nightwatchman**: *see* below), and *Deportees* (covered by him in 2010 in collaboration with **Outernational**).

After completing his degree, Morello moved to Los Angeles, where his musical skills received wider exposure when he joined **Lock Up** in 1988; they released their only album, *Something Bitchin' This Way Comes*, the following year, and broke up in 1990. He attained major success with **Rage Against The Machine**: its other members were rapper/vocalist **Zack de la Rocha**, whom Morello had first heard in action at a gig in L.A., bassist **Tim Commerford**, and drummer **Brad Wilk**. The band served up a potent brew of political rhetoric and a sound dominated by Morello's

distinctive guitar work; he claims to have used the same effects set-up, featuring a DigiTech whammy, plus a digital delay and wah-wah pedal, since the early days of RATM. The group achieved major success and massive sales with the three CDs they released between 1992 and 1999: De la Rocha's departure in 2000 led to their temporary disbandment, but RATM reunited seven years later, and continue to appear and record together.

In the aftermath of the break-up, Morello, Commerford, and Wilk formed **Audioslave** with vocalist **Chris Cornell** from **Soundgarden**. The band made three albums (their self-titled debut and 2005's *Out of Exile* were both platinum sellers) but came to an end shortly before RATM reformed in 2007. Morello's other major musical activity over the last decade has been his appearances as **The Nightwatchman** (an identity he has described as "my political folk alter ego"); for these, he accompanies his solo voice with an acoustic, nylon-strung guitar—in contrast to the Fender Telecaster and hybrid Kramer/EMG solid-body, amplified with Marshall and Peavey equipment, that he uses with RATM.

More Rock Sounds

N THIS FINAL section of our lead-playing chapter, we'll look at a few guitar techniques that aren't particularly hard to execute, and produce powerful (and noisy!) rock sounds. These are the **pick slide**, the **string rake**, and the use of controlled **feedback**.

Let's start with the **pick slide**—a.k.a. **pick scrape**. Loads of rock guitarists use this technique to great effect—from Jimi Hendrix to Kerry King (Slayer) and Michael "Padge" Paget (Bullet For My Valentine).

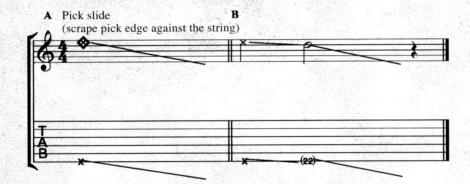

A   Pick slide
(scrape pick edge against the string)   B

Above: Sonic Youth's Thurston Moore favors *"alternative" noise-producing guitar techniques.*

The pick slide is most commonly executed by holding the pick sideways and scraping its edge along one (or two) of the wound strings, usually starting from the bridge saddle and continuing downward. You need lots of distortion for maximum effect. Example A (above) is a basic pick slide on the low E string. In example B, we have a cool variation, favored by people like Eddie Van Halen and Yngwie Malmsteen. It starts with a pick slide, and continues as a regular left-hand slide as soon as you reach the fretboard, which, in most cases, will be at fret 21 or 22. Massive sound! Be aware that pick slides often leave grooves in your pick and dramatically decrease its life span—so don't use your favorite pick every time.

Now let's look at the **string rake**, a percussive effect used by guitar greats like David Gilmour and Stevie Ray Vaughan. To perform a rake, you quickly drag (rake) the pick across one or more muted strings before hitting a note—most often in a downward motion. Rakes are generally applied in order to *accentuate* a chosen note.

This example (below) is played on the D minor pentatonic scale. We start with a rake going from your 4th string all the way down to the fretted note on the 13th fret of the 1st string. The muting can be carried out by your first, second, and third fingers, with the fourth finger fretting the 13th fret and quickly pulling off to first finger on 10th fret. Practice this slowly at first, because switching from muting to fretting requires some subtlety. Remember, we don't want to hear any actual *notes* other than the fretted ones; the muted sounds should be purely percussive. The last note is a bend preceded by another rake, this time across two strings only. Classic!

The last rock noise featured here is **feedback**. From Hendrix to Sonic Youth's Thurston Moore and Lee Ranaldo, it's been used to great effect, and is an amazing, creative, and sometimes slightly unpredictable technique…

For the example (right), put on lots of distortion, and turn up your amp a little more than usual, because these are the main ways of achieving controlled feedback. (They work especially well on tube amps.) Then play the note while turning to face the amp's loudspeaker, and slowly leaning into it. This is likely to make your guitar produce a continuous, howling note—feedback! Experiment with different settings on your guitar, and when feedback is sounding, try adding vibrato, and shaking the note with your whammy bar. There's a whole world of awesome noises to be explored…

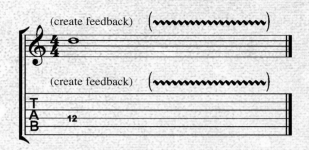

Below: Michael "Padge" Paget of Bullet For My Valentine, with his strikingly shaped ESP guitar.

Right: Noel Gallagher of Oasis, playing a Gibson ES-335.

MASTERS OF NOISE

Angus Young (AC/DC): "Stiff Upper Lip"—
   Stiff Upper Lip (2000)
Michael "Padge" Paget (Bullet For My Valentine): "Scream
   Aim Fire"—*Scream Aim Fire* (2008)
Noel Gallagher (Oasis): "Supersonic"—
   Definitely Maybe (1994)
Lee Ranaldo/Thurston Moore (Sonic Youth): "Becuz"—
   Washing Machine (1995)

Angus Young

RAKES AND PICK SLIDES

"We're a rock group. We're noisy, rowdy, sensational, and weird."

WHEN IT COMES to getting a huge crowd to rock out with you, few bands can equal flamboyant greats AC/DC. Part of the reason they do it so well lies in the showmanship of lead guitarist Angus Young. While no stranger to great percussive **rakes**, Angus also knows how to harness the power of a well-placed **pick slide**. In fact, he isn't at all afraid of using this technique quite often—and rightly so, because its electrifying, thundering sound goes well with the band's famous "lightning-bolt" logo.

Our example is based on the D minor pentatonic scale, with an extra, commonly added note for a bit of color. We start out with a large string rake from the 6th string, and move toward the two notes on the 2nd and 1st strings, which you can fret using a first finger bar. When performing the rake, use all your fingers to ensure that the muted strings make only a percussive sound, and practice the transition from muted to fretted notes until it feels manageable at high speed. Two notes played simultaneously like these are referred to as a **double-stop**. They're quite common in *Rock Guitar*, as well as in blues, which is a big part of Angus's influences.

The last part of the first bar is another double-stop: fingering-wise, I suggest using your fourth finger on the 1st string and your third on the 2nd string. Give it a nice wide vibrato, and feel the power!

Bar two features a rake across the two lowest strings, and a phrase played best with your first and third fingers; add a nice vibrato to the second note. It's followed by the classic **pick slide to regular slide** combination, as previously described. This momentous slide lands on a D power chord, which you can play with an open 4th string and your first finger fretting the 2nd fret of the 3rd string. Give the chord some extra "vibe" by adding vibrato to the note on the 2nd fret. The final bar starts with another huge rake across four strings. It continues with a cool descending phrase, going down the scale using pull-offs on each string, and culminating in another very popular double-stop, which you can bar with your first finger—adding that classic, wide rock vibrato as icing on the cake.

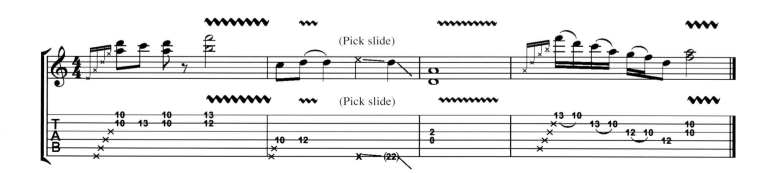

88

Aussie veterans **AC/DC—"Acca-Dacca"** to some fans—certainly qualify as "hardy perennials" in the world of rock! Brothers and fellow-guitarists **Angus** and **Malcolm Young** established the band back in 1973, and it was a year later that Angus, born in 1955, first appeared onstage in his famous "schoolboy" uniform. It made a much greater impact on audiences than any of the previous outfits he'd worn for live gigs (including "Superman" and "Spiderman" costumes), and has recently been displayed at Melbourne Museum as part of an exhibition of items associated with the city, whose St Kilda suburb was the group's base during their early years. Vocalist **Bon Scott** featured alongside Angus and Malcolm on AC/DC's debut LP, *High Voltage* (1975): the other core members, drummer **Phil Rudd** and bassist **Cliff Williams**, joined in 1975 and 1977 respectively.

The group's rising international status was confirmed by the success of *Highway to Hell* (1979)—though Bon Scott's death (from alcoholic poisoning in London on February 19, 1980) occurred before the album reached its commercial zenith. His replacement by a British ex-glam-rocker, **Brian Johnson**, was initially a surprise; however, Scott himself had admired Johnson's singing, and the newcomer's gutsy delivery proved to be a perfect match for Angus Young's hard-riffing, wonderfully raucous guitar work.

Aside from the loss of Scott, the only other serious difficulty faced by AC/DC during their lengthy career was the dismissal of Phil Rudd in 1983, precipitated by the drummer's personal problems. Rudd's place was taken by **Simon Wright** and (later) **Chris Slade**, but he rejoined the band in 1991, and Angus, Malcolm, Brian, Cliff, and Phil's joint status as hard-rock royalty is now in no doubt. Only **Michael Jackson's** *Thriller* has sold more copies worldwide than *Back in Black*, AC/DC's first post-Bon Scott album, released in 1980; and their sound, though essentially unaltered for decades, is immensely powerful and instantly recognizable. At its heart is Angus Young's trademark Gibson SG solid-body, and the guitarist is a long-time devotee of Marshall amplification.

TAKING IT FURTHER
Pedals and Effects

I N THIS CLOSING chapter, we're going to look at the further steps you can take toward becoming an original wizard of Rock Guitar! Let's start by investigating some of the effects gizmos you may want to consider in your quest for that amazing personal sound. Effects can be added via foot pedals ("stompboxes") or rackmounts—and even computer software is sometimes used.

Distortion/Overdrive

A distortion or overdrive pedal will boost the input signal from your guitar, creating an overloaded sound supplying "bite" plus lots more sustain. To hear what this kind of effect can deliver, listen to Limp Bizkit's Wes Borland on "My Generation" (*Chocolate Starfish and the Hot Dog Flavored Water*, 2000), and Sune Rose Wagner (from The Raveonettes) on "Attack of the Ghost Riders" (*Whip It On*, 2002).

Reverb

Reverberation (to give it its full name) is what occurs when a sound generates little echoes that slowly fade away. There are many kinds of reverb effect, most of them digitally generated these days: **room reverb** and **hall reverb** (which recreate the reflections encountered in indoor areas), and simulations of classic analog studio effects like **plate reverb** and **spring reverb**: they can all add a really cool sense of "space" to your sound. Check out Romy Madley Croft's use of reverb on "Islands" (from The xx's self-titled debut album, 2009), and Jason Becker's "Blue" (*Perspective*, 1995).

Delay/Echo

A delay—or echo—unit basically records your input signal and then plays it back. You can make it repeat a phrase multiple times at various speeds, and produce many other intriguing effects. For a taste of delay, try The Edge (U2) on "With or Without You" (*The Joshua Tree*, 1987)…and my own "City Echoes" (Quist—*City Echoes*, 2011).

Left: *A pedalboard mounted with a wide range of "stompboxes," that are turned on and off by the guitarist's feet as the required effects are selected. Each pedal usually generates a single effect and is operated by a simple footswitch.*

Above: Guitarist Mike Einziger of Incubus performs in Santa Barbara, California. Note his pedalboard packed with a wide variety of effects.

Chorus

Chorusing mixes your guitar's input signal with one (or more) delayed, pitch-modulated copies of itself; there are famous examples of what can result from this on Prince and The Revolution's "Purple Rain" (*Purple Rain*, 1984), and Nirvana's "Smells Like Teen Spirit" (*Nevermind*, 1991).

Wah Wah

The wah-wah pedal varies the tone and timbre of your input signal with each move of the foot, creating a distinctive effect, which sounds quite similar to the human voice pronouncing the word "wah!" It's a favorite with funk and soul players, but for classic rock wah-wah usage, you can't do better than Frank Zappa's "Willie The Pimp" (*Hot Rats*, 1969), Eric Clapton's "White Room" (*24 Nights*, 1991), or "Cotopaxi" from The Mars Delta's *Octahedron* (2009), featuring John Frusciante and Omar Rodríguez-López.

Whammy Pedal

A whammy pedal uses digital technology to shift the pitch of a played note by a selected interval (commonly one or two octaves). Whammy-pedal meisters include Audioslave's Tom Morello ("Like a Stone," *Audioslave*, 2002), and Pink Floyd's David Gilmour ("Marooned," *The Division Bell*, 1994).

Other Effects

Other effects you may want to consider include **tremolo**, **octave**, and **compression/sustain**. The latter is especially useful should you decide to have a go at playing with a **slide finger**, like the great Duane Allman. Talking of sustain, also check out the **Ebow**, a hand-held device favored by David Gilmour, The Edge, and many others. It produces a magnetic field that makes strings sound as though they are being played with a violin bow, and presents loads of musical possibilities.

There really is a vast array of effects out there, but it's worth remembering that when you connect up several pedals in a single "loop" your overall sound quality may suffer, as many devices "steal" a little bit of the guitar's signal even when they're switched off. So look out for ones that boast "true bypass:" these won't affect your sound at all when you aren't using them.

Modifications

Above: Some tools of the rock guitarist's trade, plus a few other essentials.

NOW LET'S LOOK at some of the modifications ("mods") you could consider making to your guitar. Whether you want to get closer to that killer tone, produce cool, crazy-sounding effects, help your instrument stay in tune, or simply prevent it from falling off when you're playing, "mods" are the way to improve and personalize it.

Changing Pickups

Your guitar's pickups, whether they're **single-coils** or **humbuckers** (the latter contain twin electromagnetic coils, deliver a higher output signal, and are wired so they reject or "buck" hum and buzz), are what feed the vibrations of its strings to your ears, and those of the world; so replacing them can truly transform its sound! There are really no rules about which to choose, so go ahead and experiment. Many major suppliers provide audio samples of their pickups on their websites, so you can listen before you buy and install them. Get your new pickups fitted by an expert if you aren't skilled with electrical circuits and a soldering iron.

Adding a Whammy-Bar System

Let's say you've bought an amazing vintage Fender Strat—but then realize you want to be able to produce wild, screaming dive-bombs…Well, get a top-notch modern whammy-bar system fitted! This is also a job for a specialist, because it usually involves drilling new holes, and really precise setting-up afterward.

Installing a Killswitch

"Killswitches" (or toggle switches) abruptly turn the signal from your guitar on or off. They aren't complicated to install, and some guitars already have everything you need to create a killswitch effect. My Fender Jazzmaster contains separate "lead" and "rhythm" circuits, and after turning the latter's volume to zero, I'm able to use the instrument's two-way switch to flick between its silenced "rhythm" circuit and the loud "lead" circuit. Very cool and loads of fun! To hear a killswitch in use, check out Buckethead's "King James" (*Crime Slunk Scene*, 2006); Kiss's Ace Frehley on "Cold Gin" (*Alive!*, 1975); and Tom Morello (Rage Against the Machine) playing "Know Your Enemy" (*Rage Against the Machine*, 1992).

Changing Machine Heads

Changing your guitar's machine heads (tuners) can greatly improve its tuning stability. You simply won't stay in tune while bending or using your whammy bar heavily without a good tuning system. Getting "locking" tuners is a good start.

Talking of tuning…it may also be worthwhile taking your guitar to a specialist and having it "set up" properly, ensuring that the tuning is correct all over the neck, and that the "action" —the distance between the strings and the fretboard—is exactly as you want it. Low action makes a guitar less of an effort to play, but tends to generate unwanted fret buzz; higher action gets rid of this, but is harder on your fingers. Sometimes a simple change of its action can make an instrument feel a thousand times easier and more fun to use.

Changing String Gauges

Using a different string gauge will also affect your guitar sound. Where "09" string sets—0.09 inches is the diameter of the 1st (top E) string on these—generally give you a brighter, more twangy sound and feel easy to play (and bend!), "011s," with a 1st string measuring 0.11 inches, feel much tougher on your fingers, but will reward you with a warmer, more sustained tone. Changing the gauge of your strings will usually mean having to get the guitar "set up" again to adjust to the new levels of tension.

Adding Strap Locks

Ever dropped your guitar because the strap detached itself? I know I have, and sometimes in quite dramatic (and awkwardly funny) situations! A strap lock is a simple, fairly inexpensive mechanism, but it can prevent accidents, and enable you to concentrate on the music, rather than worrying about health, safety, and broken guitars!

Musical Development

THERE ARE MANY ways to develop the skills you have achieved so far and to expand your musicality further. A few of the most effective are outlined here…

Learn the Music of Your Heroes

One of my favorite things to do when growing up was studying the music of the guitar players I admired—their riffs, their solos, anything that took my fancy. Most of the time, I'd rely on nothing but *listening* to the recorded music (Tabs were expensive!), and some tracks would take me *ages* to master, as I had to listen to one tiny bit at a time. However, I loved it—because I always chose to learn stuff I was totally mad about. Today, I'm very grateful, because these listening projects did wonders for the development of my "ear!" Try it—it'll do wonders for your musical capability.

Jam Along to Records

Another thing I did a lot when I was learning the guitar was to play along to records. I recommend trying to jam with blues records for a start, because you need just one scale, and can concentrate on "soaking" up the vibes from the record.

Make Your Own Backing Tracks

Put together a recorded backing track to jam with, featuring one chord progression for each scale you want to practice, strummed to a "click" track (an electronic metronome beat to keep you in strict tempo) for five minutes. Get an experienced guitarist/musician to help you come up with the chord sequences. This will provide loads of musical fun, while helping you to get to know your scales.

Consider Getting a Teacher

A good guitar teacher will make you practice, and regularly set goals to meet. Find someone knowledgeable and experienced enough to help you with the pieces and techniques you can't work out yourself—and who can open up the doors to the realm of music theory.

Find Other People to Play With

Making music with like-minded people is so much fun, and the feeling you get when you're part of a band that plays well together is…well, one of the best sensations I can think of! Go experience it now, if you haven't already.

Left: Michael "Padge" Paget, whose band Bullet For My Valentine are part of a new generation of British heavy-metal bands.

Right: All-female heavy metal band Hysterica come from Stockholm, Sweden. Following their first European tour in 2009, they won the award for Best Newcomer in the Swedish Metal Awards in 2010.

Opposite top: Soundgarden—one of many top rock bands who owe their success to years of work and steady practice.

Get the Most Out of Practicing

Be disciplined. Learn one thing at a time. In a good practice session, you should mix the fun stuff with things you find a little harder, and know you need to improve.

Practice regularly. One hour a day for seven days is better then seven hours once a week.

Practice slooooowly. The irony is that the slower you're willing to practice, the faster you'll be likely to learn. Practicing too fast means your brain doesn't get enough time to take things in properly, and it also allows bad habits (wrong notes, unwanted strings ringing) to become integral parts of your playing.

Get a metronome. And use it for at least *some* of the time you practice (e.g. for scales). Not only will this help you develop that all-important *sense of rhythm*, it's also a great way to track your progress, and challenge yourself and set some goals in terms of speed. But remember, start slowly—and never move on before you can play the chosen scale or piece perfectly every time.

Transpose everything. Move your scales, exercises, songs, etc. around the keys. For example, once you've mastered starting the major scale from the A on the 5th fret of the 6th string, try starting it from the A# on the 6th fret! Also, relate the scales to the CAGED system, because this will help you to learn them all over the fretboard. Then practice playing them in sequences… the possibilities are endless.

Most Importantly: Have Fun!

That's it, folks. Now please *remember to have fun!* Learn the songs, riffs, solos, and techniques that you absolutely love. That way, learning and playing the guitar will *never* be a waste of time, and you'll keep the flame burning—and get more and more excited by your own awesome achievements.

Enjoy!

Index